VHS
ATE MY
BRAIN II:
THE REVENGE

VHS ATE MY BRAIN II:
THE REVENGE

By Andrew Hawnt

This book is dedicated to my sons, Alex and Joe.
As is my life.

VHS ATE MY BRAIN II: THE REVENGE
Table of contents
(No page numbers. After all, VHS didn't have chapters!)

Introduction: The Revenge

Photo by Rob Lane

I love sequels.

They usually have more special effects, crazier stories and louder explosions. Even the sequels that went straight to video without the stars of the original get me excited. I want to know what happens next.

In 2014 I put out a book called *VHS Ate My Brain*. I put a revised edition of that book out in 2023 (*VHS Ate My Brain: Revised Edition*, which was almost double the length of the original), but there's still more to say. Why am I writing a new volume after ten years?

The original, much to my surprise and delight, has endured for a decade and is still finding new readers. The

VHS scene didn't just grow - it blossomed. So this new volume is intended as a look at the intervening years since the VHS scene emerged from its secret hideout, what may lay ahead for the VHS collecting hobby and a gathering of interviews with current elements of the VHS nostalgia boom.

A lot has happened since the original came out. So let's catch up with an old friend, stick some tapes on, and find out what happened next. The first book told my story, how video tapes and video stores gave me solace as well as entertainment. It then moved on to how I discovered that I wasn't alone in my fascination with the little plastic boxes filled with magnetic tape. That there was actually a gigantic network of people around the planet who shared in my love for the format and the memories that came with it.

This time I want to talk about what the VHS scene has become and how perceptions of it have changed. Yeah, we still see the 'THIS VHS TAPE IS WORTH A HUNDRED GRAND" type news pieces from time to time, but on the whole, the resurgence of interest in VHS and the video era has wound up directly influencing modern pop culture, from *Stranger Things* to Synthwave, the glitchy VHS aesthetic and more. I'll also be looking at some of the great - and not-so-great - sequels of thc video era.

Recently I came across an intriguing-looking film called *Videoman* on Amazon Prime. The poster image showed a guy being apparently absorbed by a TV, which immediately conjured images in my head of *Videodrome* style body horror and weird alternate dimensions. I hit play on it and was surprised, even a little shocked, to see someone very much like me on the screen. I mean scarily so. The

Videoman in question is a middle-aged bald guy who wears slogan t-shirts and black hoodies, obsesses over genre films and lives in a basement full of VHS. Okay, I live in suburbia rather than a basement full of tapes, but the rest is pretty accurate, as is his grumpy demeanour.

This Swedish film, written and directed by Kristian A. Söderström, is a darkly comic look at two individuals - a VHS collector and a woman obsessed with the 80s - dealing with the stresses of modern life in their own ways. There's a missing VHS tape drama involved as well. The nerdy collector element naturally spoke to me, as did the unexpectedly emotional side of the film. Seeing the VHS guy coping with life's weirdnesses and anxieties by getting lost in movie trivia and watching graphic exploitation films (often with a parade of like-minded ultra-awkward nerds), I felt a deeper sense of kinship. Aside from the obvious baldy in black t-shirts thing, his reliance on things from the past to give his present some focus and meaning struck a chord with me.

Why am I so interested in old films and TV shows? Why aren't I binging everything that streaming services fling out at me? Am I just getting old and craving the familiar, or is there something else going on? What am I getting out of revelling in the old?

It's quite telling that I found the VHS basement in *Videoman* quite comforting. The rows of tapes, magazines, movie posters and shelving units spoke to my sense of order in the things I love, the need to display them in a certain way so I can enjoy them properly.

It also chimes with my recent explorations into getting a formal diagnosis for my very, very obvious neurodivergence. The signs have been there my whole life, but in recent years I have come to understand more about the condition. That feeling of everything falling into place has been quite profound. It explains my oddly wired brain very well. It explains why I couldn't see my way out of a job that I hated and which ruined my life for nine years. It's why I found myself in some very strange and painful situations that I never really understood.

We're all learning more about ourselves each day, be it in good ways or ways that send you on a spiral of soul-searching and learning, so a little escapism has been a massive help. This is especially so for me through the bouts of depression, the stress of parenting, of working full time, of trying - and failing miserably - to maintain a social life. When I am at my lowest, I know I can slide the doors open on my film library like that bit in *Hot Fuzz*. By the power of Greyskull!

I spoke in the previous volume of *VHS Ate My Brain* about how movies became an escape for me from the troubled and often dangerous area I lived in as a teenager, and how as I grew up they took on an even deeper meaning. Here and now I see that films also help to centre me and cut through the mental chaos. If I'm watching a film, I can push the anxiety and worry and stress and overactive mind aside for 90 minutes.

A lot has changed since I put the first book out, but a lot has remained the same. I don't haunt the social media groups much any more as they could get a bit much to deal with thanks to warring factions and the usual online tendency to just flame each other for the hell of it.

I still go retro hunting like I always have, but these days the hauls include DVDs, books, comics and a heck of a lot of retro T-shirts rather than tapes. I miss being able to come across awesome ex-rental tapes every week, but times change and things move and evolve.

Do I still love tapes to an unhealthy degree? Hell yes. Has my interest diminished since the original book? No, but my available time, space and disposable income have. The kids are way bigger now and way more demanding of my resources. The house isn't big enough for a giant collection any more. I have to be more selective, but that's okay really as it stops me from buying any old junk. I have more focus now. I admit that at several points during the life of my old collection I bought tapes for the sake of it. The hoarder thing kicked in and I would snap up almost anything, but that passed. Thankfully.

My love for VHS, ten years on from the book that changed my life, is still here. I'm older, happier and on a better journey than before.

I guess you could say I sorted out my tracking. I think we all do eventually.

It's good to be back.

Chapter One
Welcome back to the video shop

You see the sign in the distance, the trusty logo looking a bit rough around the edges these days, but still, the excitement builds as soon as you see it. You arrive at the door and it feels familiar and reassuring as you open it and the bottom hinge squeaks at a pitch you've heard a thousand times. Maybe more.

You walk inside and immediately you're in your happy place. A trailer tape plays on a loop at the counter at the other end of the store. You've arrived just as a trailer for an action movie ends with two guys running away from an explosion. Under that, you can hear the low but atmospheric sounds of film soundtrack songs playing over the store stereo, speakers hidden behind bright standees of upcoming releases and faded standees of old favourites. To your right is the largest area of the store, where the latest releases are lined up loud and proud on the custom video shop wall shelves, perfectly spaced out with the tapes at a slight angle so everything is visible as soon as you walk in.

To your left is the slightly-less-recent releases section, a little room of its own, where titles that have moved out of the new release shelves to a new home and sporting new, slightly lower, prices on their rental stickers.

You nod a greeting to the lady behind the counter, and she returns it cheerfully. You're well known in the shop. She probably already knows what you'll rent. She's adding more rolled-up posters to the box by the counter where they sell the old promos for small change. Sometimes they put your name on the back of posters you ask about so you can buy them the next time you're in. They're cool like that there. The racks of snacks and drinks are looking well stocked too. The shop is ready for a busy weekend of renting tapes and selling savoury and sweet sustenance along with a beverage of your choice.

In the corner, by the front end of the new release racks, there are two wire bins filled with tapes that have reached the end of their rental life. The shop is selling those at two quid a pop, and you know you'll have a look before you leave.

You go and browse the new releases first. Then it'll be the smaller room before your favourite section upstairs. Save the best for last. You look through the big-name releases with big stars on their covers and review straplines from tabloid newspapers, rich in hyperbole.

Beneath the big releases are the latest straight-to-video offerings, and that's where your heart lies. Low-budget horror movies, lowbrow science fiction sequels and allegedly high-octane martial arts action flicks are on offer. You take a look at the covers, the blurbs on the back cover, the companies that put them out, the casts and even the running time. 85-90 minutes is your personal sweet spot, as it's easy to fit two films that length into one night's viewing.

Those new releases are overnight rental only, so you'd need to come back the next day. You don't really mind doing that, as it's an excuse to carry out the ritual of the three rooms all over again if the mood takes you.

It's a tough decision to pick a new title, so you decide to visit the room beside it and see what has slipped into a slightly more budget status. Lots of titles have already had their time in your player and have their names proudly recorded on your account card behind the counter. Nothing is really jumping out at you in that section that you haven't already seen, so you head back to the new releases and pick a horror movie, a sci-fi movie and a martial arts title. The choice is hard, as the horror is a sequel you want to see, the sci-fi has a killer cyborg in it and the martial arts film stars your favourite low-budget ass-kicker.

Eventually, you decide on the horror sequel, because you love sequels. You put the other two back into their slots on the shelving, leaving one exposed empty shelf where the sequel you're clutching was. The lady behind the counter raises one corner of her mouth, She knew you'd go for that.

New release in hand, it's time to go upstairs to the promised land. You head to the staircase that separates the two downstairs rooms and savour each step, the walls of the staircase thickly decorated with layers of movie posters from every genre and every echelon of the film industry.

You never really notice what colour the carpet is on the stairs across the years you visit the shop as you're always fascinated by the posters on the walls and - deliciously - the ceiling as well. It's like traversing a portal into a dimension of lost films and you never tire of it.

The upstairs room opens up before you, its musty aroma is oddly comforting. There are no windows, just some strip lights and a whole lot of VHS rental boxes. The walls are loosely arranged into genres, but towards the back of the room, it all goes to hell with the tapes it would be hard to classify.

Upstairs, it's two films for £1 for three nights. These are the old tapes, the weird tapes, the cult movies that found an audience long after they faded from the consciousness of the masses. There are classics in there too, evergreen films that will always get a rental now and again, no matter how dated they are.

You slowly make your way around the room, doing your usual full circuit before you inevitably settle on the sections with the horror movies, sci-fi and 80s comedies. You decide that, as you already have a horror movie for the night, that a sci-fi flick and a comedy are the way to go for the other two tapes you're going to rent. You'll fit two in tonight, likely the horror first and then the sci-fi, followed by the comedy when you eventually wake up.

You're addicted to the joys of the shop. It's a beautiful feeling to be able to rent some escapism from the things that are bugging you. The dangers of the area you live in. Money. Health. Family stuff. The future. Your fragile mental state. With a few tapes under your arm, you know you can take the night off from the stress you have been fighting all week.

Three tapes have now been chosen, but you do another circuit of the upstairs room just in case you missed something the first time around. You've seen so many things in that room that a lot of the tapes feel like landmarks, little markers from past scenes of your life. You've watched so many films in the past few years that you have started to see days as scenes, the music you love acting as a soundtrack to your origin story before the third act begins and things start happening. It could be worse. There are far worse vices to have. So what if you're weird.

Much later in life, you may find out why you're weird and it'll change everything about how you see your life and the things you have been through, but right now all you want is your fix of films.

Reluctantly you leave the room and head back downstairs. You stop by the bargain bins and find a couple of tapes you had rented years ago going cheap. You add those to your pile so you can buy them and rescue them from the horrible fate of going home with someone other than you. That just wouldn't be acceptable.

You sit your stack on the counter and add a bag of chocolate snacks, a bag of savoury snacks and two cans of pop. There's a pizza in the freezer at home. You should be set for the night. You make small talk with the staff member as she puts stuff through the till. You hand over your membership card and she notes the rentals against your account. You unroll a carrier bag from your coat pocket and fill it with tapes and snacks. A quick look in the box of used promo posters brings up a sci-fi sequel poster. The edges

14

are a bit frayed with pin holes but it's definitely worth the 25p you pay for it.

Eventually, you leave, oblivious to the fact that you've been in there for over an hour and it's starting to go dark.

You wish you could spend every day there but you never get up the courage to ask about any jobs going there. You regret not doing so for years to come especially when one day you revisit your home town after moving away from it and you find the video shop is long gone, replaced by a nail bar that also closes a few months later.

But that's the future. Right now you're carrying a bag with a great night ahead. It makes you think of the nights you would spend with your dad, going to the video shop, getting fish and chips and staying up into the middle of the night talking nonsense. You miss those days.

You walk home, avoiding the houses where the dangerous people live. You get the pizza in the oven and make small talk with your mum before heading up to the safe haven of your bedroom, its walls lined with books, VHS tapes, posters, photos and postcards. You shut the curtains and turn on the lamp rather than the main light as it's more atmospheric. You get comfy on your bed, a pizza on a tray beside you and the acquisitions from the video shop on the other side.

You hit play on the remote and you're whisked away.

A lifetime later you end up writing a book about VHS tapes and going to video shops. Soon you start receiving messages from people around the world and discover you were never alone. There were hundreds, maybe thousands, maybe more out there, just like you. People finding solace in tapes and closing the curtains to block out the world.

People who, for 90 minutes at a time, could find happiness.

Chapter Two
Sequels: Bigger, louder, faster!

This is a sequel, so of course I need to talk about sequels. What is it that I find so endearing about them? Why do I keep coming back for more when in many cases they're just more of the same or simply tarnish the original? Some sequels break that tradition and wind up being the definitive piece of a franchise (*Star Wars Episode V: The Empire Strikes Back* and *Star Trek II: The Wrath of Khan*, for two easily recognisable examples). If those first sequels brought in money, then you could pretty much guarantee that, at least in genre movies, you would get a sequel before too long.

But then what? With more sequels come more changes. Cast and crew move on, eventually leaving those franchises that went on for far too many entries, resulting in productions that barely resemble the originals aside from their titles.

I freely admit that many sequels miss the mark quite spectacularly, but the thing I loved about them right from my formative years of watching things that were far too grown up for me was the chance to hang out in those universes again. I needed the escapism.

There are franchises where sequels have turned them into something of a joke. Take the *Fast And The Furious* series of films for example. At the time of writing, there are ten movies in the main series and one spinoff (the watchable action flick *Hobbs and Shaw*, featuring Dwayne 'the Rock' Johnson and Jason Statham in the dual lead roles). The number of sequels is only outdone by the number of times 'family' is mentioned. They're all pretty entertaining (and increasingly silly), but the sheer number of them is ridiculous.

It was the same in the VHS era, with beloved franchises like *A Nightmare on Elm Street, Friday the 13th* and *Halloween* pumping sequels out until audiences just gave up on them.

Then at the other end of the quality spectrum, and I mean a long, long way away from those classic franchises, you have dreck like the *Witchcraft* movies. How many of those are there now? Seventeen? I've lost track. Those films survived so long directly because of their status as sequels to something vaguely recognisable, and not down to the quality of the films. Actually, the amount of gratuitous nudity in them probably kept them in rentals for a good long while as well.

While often creatively impotent, sequels come with a built-in audience and may be seen as less of a gamble for studios to make. Brand familiarity can go a long way, and if a title can maintain its audience, you can bet there'll be more of them until that audience dwindles.

I'll get to some of the franchises whose sequels nearly ended them a little later.

It wasn't just studios that saw sequels as a safe bet in the VHS era. They were also attractive to rental stores for the same reason. If a tape was pretty much guaranteed an audience, they knew they would make back the initial outlay of the cost of the tapes. Once they had paid for themselves, those tapes would go on to earn those stores a profit. That return was a big deal to video store owners and could help their businesses tick over in lean periods. Displaying the whole series of films in a franchise was attractive on the shelves and, I would imagine, encouraged customers to rent them all.

It was an idea that certainly worked for me. I ate sequels up whenever I could get hold of them, and I'm not sure if it's down to loving the originals, completism or my emerging neurodivergence that went undiagnosed for so long. It's likely all of the above. Over the years this has made me wonder which of them I really enjoyed and which I ate up just because I couldn't let myself have an incomplete set of them in my head. The last decade since the original *VHS Ate My Brain* has brought with it a lot of personal revelations in terms of the way my brain works and why things panned out the way they did in my life for so long.

Without going into too much detail, I don't think I knew how to be a functioning member of society. I always felt like an outsider in a human suit, trying to keep up with what was socially acceptable but never quite hitting the mark. Here in the distant future, I understand that this was a manifestation of my faulty wiring, but at the time it was a frustrating mess.

All of which made my obsession with films and TV shows on VHS tapes more intense, so sequels were perfect things for me. I've lost track of all of the sequels I have ingested over the years, and aside from aberrations like *Wishmaster 3: Devil Stone* and *Wishmaster 4: The Prophecy Fulfilled,* I've loved pretty much all of them in some way.

What follows is a selection of video-era sequels that I believe are worth revisiting. Sequels by their nature can be easy money for the studios that make them as there's a ready-made audience. They often don't have to work as hard to find people to watch them.

In some cases, they widen the audience, but in the video era, they often played to increasingly small audiences, depending on how far down the well the franchises went. That said, there were some great sequels available to enjoy.

As my focus was always horror, sci-fi and martial arts action movies, those are the focus here. These are all sequels I feel have merit and warrant a rewatch. Some may be obvious, but some may be new to you. Mainly the inspiration here is to nerd out over tapes. I mean, I'm pretty fond of doing that.

Chapter 3
Sequels that did the trick

The video era was awash with sequels, far outnumbering remakes and reboots. I would argue that this promoted more creativity, even though some franchises stagnated. Presented here is a selection of rental store-era sequels that got the job done. Many will disagree with my opinions on these movies, and I'm totally cool with that. We like different stuff. I'd love to hear your picks for sequels that worked well, so do hit me up on social media if I can still force myself to use it by the time you read this.

Fright Night Part 2 (1988)
The first *Fright Night* was fun, but for me, it was the sequel that was the better film. The new villains were more rounded, the comedy/horror mix was sharper and it had Roddy McDowell firing on all cylinders as the vampire-hunting horror host Peter Vincent again teams up with teen Charlie Brewster to take on a horde of evildoers. This one feels much more immediate than its predecessor and it gallops along at a great pace. As well as getting the comedy right, there are several great effects shots, especially the final fate of the vampire queen at the climax.

Pumpkinhead II: Blood Wings (1994)

The original *Pumpkinhead* was released over here as *Vengeance the Demon* if I remember rightly, and while that had its moments, this first sequel was a far superior film. The franchise had found its feet with this one, offering a stronger story and a more effective monster. The Pumpkinhead effects were excellent, giving the demon a presence that CGI still can't achieve. *Blood Wings* has bags of atmosphere and is one of those sequels that enriches the world of the first film rather than damages it.

Warlock: The Armageddon (1993)
The original *Warlock* movie was a full-on cinema release starring Richard E Grant facing off against the late Julian Sands as the titular Warlock. It was hokey and a bit silly and wasn't a huge hit, but it garnered enough attention to warrant a sequel. Two actually, but *Warlock: The Armageddon* was way better than the belated third, which didn't star Sands in it. This first sequel upped the gothic weirdness, and while the effects have dated a great deal, it remains a compelling watch.

Cyborg 2: Glass Shadow (1993)
I loved this film from the first time I rented it, and not just because it starred a young Angelina Jolie and I was an impressionable teenager. It also starred Elias Koteas (Casey Jones from the original *Teenage Mutant Ninja Turtles* movie) and bits of Jack Palance's face while he's being mysterious from a screen. What I liked about this is that, despite it being a low-budget sci-fi actioner that went straight to video, it acts like a far bigger film in its approach

23

to things like cinematography and scale. A surprisingly fun watch.

Robocop 2 (1990)
When I saw the original 1987 *Robocop* movie from Paul Verhoeven, I was instantly hooked. It was visceral, exciting, brutal, funny and like nothing else around. The 1990 sequel, directed by Irvin Kirshner (the guy who directed *The Empire Strikes Back*) brings back Peter Weller as Robocop and Nancy Allen as Lewis in an adventure that is, well, very 1990.

The grimy punch of the original is replaced by a slightly more sanitised aesthetic, and while the story often veers away from Robocop himself, the rest of the cast holds things together pretty well. Some excellent use of stop-motion animation in the robot fights was a highlight with this one. Nowhere near the classic that the original is, but it's still a hundred times better than *Robocop 3…*

Return of the Living Dead 3 (1993)
Now here's a great example of a sequel that does a lot of stuff right. While nothing will ever top the original 1985 *Return of the Living Dead* for its crazy punk rock atmosphere, humour, ludicrous effects and infamous dance sequences starring Linnea Quigley, *ROTLD 3* (directed by none other than Brian Yuzna) is still fun.

Not as silly as the first or as disjointed as the second, it takes a different approach to zombies and the Trioxin gas. Melinda Clarke plays Julie, who dies in an accident. Her horrified boyfriend takes her to his dad's workplace -

namely a military lab where Trioxin is being used to experiment on captive zombies. Julie is resurrected with the gas, but at what cost? The film follows her journey as she fights to retain her humanity while the Trioxin transforms her into a powerful killing machine.

The humour is much more subdued this time out, but thanks to a great young cast and some very clever direction, you end up feeling genuine pathos for Julie in her plight. Plus, when her various body modifications are complete, there's an absolutely iconic shot as she is revealed in her final form. A quality sequel made on a low budget. See, it can be done! I told you so!

Basket Case 2 (1990)

The first *Basket Case* is one of my favourite horror movies ever. Actually, it was one of my first-ever rentals. The grindhouse feel of it pulled me in straight away. This sequel, released eight years after the original, was again written and directed by Frank Henenlotter. When the original creator is involved, sequels always feel like they have a bit more legitimacy to me. Also returning is Kevin VanHentenryk as Duane, the man who had been hiding his deformed psychotic twin, Belial, in the titular basket.

The grindhouse feel is gone, replaced by a slicker production that showcases some spectacular practical effects when Duane and Belial find themselves taken into a home for wildly creative genetic oddities. It's a very different film to the first one and the rubber mutants may be hard for some viewers to take seriously due to the outlandish nature of their designs, but it's certainly worth revisiting, if only to see the depravity that Henenlotter shows with such obvious delight.

I struggled to like *Basket Case 3* that followed in 1991, which is weird as - as far as I've been able to ascertain - they were shot back to back. I think that, after watching *Basket Case 2*, that second sequel took the story too far away from the grimy darkness of the original. So while the series ended on a less-than-stellar note, the first sequel deserves a chance.

Hellbound: Hellraiser II (1988)
Hellbound is like the Rolls-Royce of horror sequels. The original *Hellraiser* is a genuine classic, but it's rare that fans ever get a sequel to anything on the level of this. Bringing back Ashley Laurence's Kirsty gives the film some continuity with its predecessor, even though this one is played on a grander scale. Kirsty finds herself in an institute, but rather than finding help there she finds someone obsessed with bringing the Cenobites back, with horrific results.

Directed by Tony Randel, *Hellbound: Hellraiser II* ups the ante in terms of gore and elaborate set pieces, but it's not just more eye candy for the sake of it, The script and visuals further enrich the Hellraiser lore, bringing an edge of surrealism to the franchise that was never really repeated through the many sequels that came after this one.

There are visuals in this film that really freaked me out when I first saw them, such as the weird things erupting from Dr Channard's fingers after his transformation into a hellish Cenobite himself. The finger effects were achieved with stop-motion animation, which always has an uncanny

26

look anyway. It really added to the cosmic horror weirdness of it all.

Something wonderful about *Hellbound* is that things aren't all explained, instead opting for some elements to remain ambiguous. This really works in its favour, as do unsettling visuals like the weird yet imposing Leviathan, hanging in the air above an infernal maze.

Hellbound is a fantastic example of a sequel building on the original in the best way.

Critters 2: The Main Course (1988)

The original *Critters* was a ton of fun, featuring carnivorous alien furballs intent on destruction in Kansas being chased down by shapeshifting bounty hunters from space. It was ridiculous, scratching that itch that *Gremlins* had created (*Gremlins 2: The New Batch* wouldn't arrive until 1990) in the best way.

This first sequel of three is a direct follow-up, featuring much of the cast from the original and the return of the bounty hunters and their spectacularly eighties futurist outfits and haircuts. It's louder, bigger and more chaotic than the first film and takes less time to get going, but somehow it manages to also ramp up the entertainment factor as well. It's gloriously silly, hammy and cheap, but it excels at being a fun flick, and that counts for a lot.

This one was followed by *Critters 3*, which famously featured a very young Leonardo Dicaprio, but which was nowhere near as fun.

Reanimator 2 aka Bride of Reanimator (1990)

The first *Reanimator* movie is an absolute blast, filled with sinister experiments, gore and reanimated corpses, all topped off with the gloriously odd performance by Jeffrey Combs as Herbert West.

Reanimator 2 (known as *Bride of Reanimator* in some territories) ups the horror when Herbert sets about building his perfect woman. It feels a little more campy than the original but delivers the shocks and the red stuff admirably.

The original was directed by Stuart Gordon, while this sequel was helmed by Brian Yuzna. The change in directors works well here, with Yuzna really getting into the schlocky spirit of this Lovecraftian delight.

Star Trek VI: The Undiscovered Country (1991)
After the truly awful fifth film in the series (*Star Trek V: The Final Frontier*), it looked like the *Star Trek* feature film series was at its lowest ebb, but this 1991 follow-up is a completely different prospect. This was the last *Star Trek* film to feature the full original cast before the baton was handed to the *Next Generation* crew with the seventh film, *Star Trek: Generations*.

This sixth film is a note-perfect send-off for the original gang, stuffed with space battles, standoffs with Klingons, intrigue and daring escapes. While not the most original of plots, it works like a greatest hits package with all of the crew banter and majestic visuals.

Even now it holds up really well, with David Warner's performance as Chancellor Gorkon and Christopher Plummer as General Chang really giving their all in the bad guy stakes. A supremely watchable and exciting film.

28

Poltergeist II: The Other Side (1986)

1984's *Poltergeist* was packed with Spielbergian emotion and some chilling visuals from director Tobe Hooper (of *Texas Chainsaw Massacre* fame), however, the first of two sequels was a different and darker entry helmed instead by Brian Gibson. This film introduced us to the sinister Kane, a sunken-eyed preacher played by Julian Beck, bringing a creepy villain to the franchise rather than just the nameless otherworld of the original.

Instead of going for massive set pieces, *Poltergeist II: The Other Side* moves at a slower, more creepy pace. Of course, there are some set pieces, but the overall feeling is one of an oppressive darkness with little hope to be found.

This features one of the only movie moments to ever really freak me out, when Craig T Nelson's Steve Freeling character undergoes a sudden mood shift, becoming horribly frightening before vomiting up a demon. The shot where the demon is emerging from his throat has stayed with me ever since. A bit of an overlooked horror gem.

Dawn of the Dead (1978)

1978 was pretty momentous for me as it's when I was born. That great historic event aside, it was also the year that George A Romero unleashed probably the greatest horror sequel of all time in *Dawn of the Dead*. This follow-up to his seminal horror classic *Night of the Living Dead* has echoed through the ages just as much as its predecessor.

A masterpiece of tension, the movie largely takes place in a shopping mall and follows people desperately trying to survive against insurmountable odds. Just like the original film, the focus is very much on the characters trying to survive rather than the ghouls trying to devour them. That is the beauty of Romero's zombie classics - their characters are front and centre and act as the hook that pulls people into the story, which is pretty similar throughout all of them if we're honest.

Dawn of the Dead caught on in a big way and has long been cemented as a genre milestone. The zombies aren't the gloopy pizza-faced horrors of the Italian zombie flicks, instead presented as blue-skinned ghouls that still look human. That makes them more unnerving, and with the expert special effects work of Tom Savini, their violence hit hard.

The film, while dated by today's tedious digital standards, holds up as an exercise in suspense and nihilism, with its themes of hopelessness matched by the determination of its cast to survive beyond the end credits. It's time to watch it again right now. Go ahead. I'll wait.

Gremlins 2: The New Batch (1990)

Taking a step away from out-and-out horror, let's take a moment to appreciate the sheer insanity of *Gremlins 2: The New Batch*, the 1990 sequel to the 1984 hit *Gremlins.*

Both films were directed by Joe Dante, and his style is all over them. The first film played out in a pretty straightforward way, with the introduction of Gizmo the Mogwai and the dangers of getting him wet or feeding him after midnight. This one? Well, this one is deranged.

It's very much a case of everything happening all at once, with Zach Galligan and Phoebe Cates' characters from the first film returning to help try and reign things in before the world is overcome by the mad cast of mutated Gremlins.

While the first took place in a relatable town setting, this one largely takes place in one building, the technologically advanced Clamp Centre. The high-rise building setting makes for some crazy action, almost like a monster-centric *Die Hard* in places. Christopher Lee hams it up as a mad scientist too, so you know you're in for a good time.

The film plays almost like a spoof, giving the violent aspects of it a more comedic edge than the scarier original. While not as dark, it's a ridiculous amount of fun. My favourite part is still when the film literally breaks, revealing the silhouettes of the two Gremlins responsible, giggling away. It's a really clever moment of fourth wall destruction and totally in keeping with the spirit of the film. Demented but so enjoyable.

Terminator 2: Judgement Day (1991)
One film that is an obvious choice when talking about sequels that got it right has to be *T2*. Everything about this film has blockbuster written all over it. Arnold Schwarzenegger at the peak of his powers as an action star. Linda Hamilton back as Sarah Connor, now an absolute badass. Eddie Furlong showing talent as John Connor way before his issues sadly derailed his career. Hell, they even bagged a song by Guns n' Roses as the kickass single for the soundtrack (*"You Could Be Mine"*).

But beyond all of these, the film had spectacular direction from James Cameron, who only five years previously had brought the world arguably the definitive sequel of all sequels in the shape of *Aliens* in 1986. This was a James

31

Cameron eager to take the *Terminator* idea - and filmmaking technology - to whole new places. This was a James Cameron that pushed the boundaries of what cinema could do at the time in terms of effects and set pieces. This was not the James Cameron that bored the tits off me with *Avatar.*

Personally, I believe that the first *Terminator* was a better film, but I put that down to me loving its harder edge, its more nihilistic violence, the greater sense of threat from the T-800. *Terminator 2: Judgement Day* is a far less frightening film. It is, however, a far more exciting one. The original had a grimy, oily, musty sort of sci-fi feel to it, whereas its massively successful sequel went for giant explosions, huge stunts and less horror. That's not to say there aren't some disturbing visuals in it, though. After all, the iconic dream sequence in which Sarah sees herself caught in a nuclear blast is forever etched into the minds of millions of fans.

Terminator 2 succeeds as a sequel as it ramps up everything from the first film and makes it more accessible. It had a lower certificate here in the UK so more people saw it. Word of mouth and some brilliant reviews did their work and *T2* became a genuine cultural phenomenon.

The film is packed with iconic moments; every scene that features Robert Patrick's T-1000, the future war flashes, Sarah Connor showing off her combat skills, the thumb (you know the thumb I mean). It all gelled together into a perfect storm of a sequel that had audiences coming back for more again and again.

Its home video release was a huge success as well, both on the rental market and as a mass-market retail tape. To this day, *Terminator 2* is held in high regard and is yet to be topped by anything that followed it. The movie sequels that came after it have never hit the same heights or the same level of skill. The closest we got to a proper follow-up to *T2* was the short-lived TV series *Terminator: The Sarah Connor Chronicles*, which featured Lena Headey as Sarah Connor and the awesome Summer Glau (of *Firefly* fame) as a cyborg called Cameron Phillips. That show pushed the ideas of the franchise further than the movies were willing to go, but sadly only lasted two seasons.

Terminator 2: Judgement Day stands as a great action film, a great sci-fi film, a great blockbuster and a truly great sequel.

Evil Dead 2: Dead By Dawn (1987)

Sam Raimi brought a DIY punch in the face of a film to genre viewers with *The Evil Dead* in 1981, which wound up banned in the UK for seven years as part of the Video Nasties controversy. It wasn't prosecuted, but it became pretty much the most notorious of the nasties for a good long while due to the legends of its extremity.

This first sequel to the original wasn't as gory and had more humour to it, but that doesn't stop it being a far superior film. The original had been made with a tiny budget and limited resources, which added to its surreal atmosphere, but it's clear there was more coin available for this second outing.

It's a bit of a weird one in some ways, as it acts as both a remake of the original film and also a sequel to it. There are some confusing shots at the start that suggest only Ash and Linda were at the cabin, but it is supposed to take place right after the first film.

That aside, *Evil Dead 2* is an absolute classic that takes the blueprint for the first movie and makes it weirder, more outlandish and way more funny. Humour aside, it's a very effective horror film with some great gross-out moments and weirdness. For example, once Ash feels like he's losing his mind among the items in the possessed cabin, he matches the movements of a lamp which appears to be dancing, a big mad grin on his face as reality seems to break down around him.

It also takes the chainsaw glimpsed in the original to new heights, by having Ash hack off his own hand when it becomes possessed and replace it with a mount that he can attach a goddamn chainsaw to. It took the film to a new visceral high and turned Ash into a horror icon.

Evil Dead 2 doesn't waste any time in getting underway, and its urgency only becomes more pronounced as the movie's compact running time plays out. It's a film that pays for multiple rewatches, as there's often so much going on in the frame that you miss things, but those rewatches are entirely deserved and thoroughly rewarding. *Evil Dead 2* is one of the glorious rare sequels that are ten times better than their predecessor. Groovy.

Aliens (1986)

Aliens is the stuffed crust pizza of sequels. Ridley Scott's original *Alien* (1979) was a masterpiece of tension with a vein of horror running through its chilling sci-fi premise.

When James Cameron took over for this first sequel in what would become a lengthy (and increasingly poor) franchise, he amped up everything - the effects, the set pieces, the cast, the scale of it, everything. The thing is, instead of being an empty series of explosions and spectacle, the film is a masterful example of character-driven excitement.

Like John Carpenter's *The Thing* from a few years earlier, the key to the success of *Aliens* is in its cast. If any single member of the cast was of a lesser calibre, Aliens would not have been anywhere near as effective. Sigourney Weaver. Michael Biehn. Bill Paxton. Lance Henriksen. Jenette Goldstein. Everyone else. They were superb, and as ramshackle bands of colonial marines go, they couldn't have been better.

The characters are generally dicks, and that's a quick way to make them relatable as, come on, we're all dicks really, aren't we? That's why we root so hard for Hicks and Vasquez and Ripley throughout it. We care about those grimy bastards because we feel like they're *our* grimy bastards. This also makes it much more impactful when anyone is lost along the way. It hurts us as much as the characters.

The attacks are brutal and unrelenting, giving the marines that underdog feeling and making us cheer and punch the air with delight when they blow up more xenomorphs.

So much of this film is iconic, and rightly so, but the Powerloader scene is my favourite by far. This film just doesn't get old. It doesn't lose its power.

I do believe that *Aliens* is the greatest sequel ever made.

*

Other sequels that got it right - in my eyes at least - include films like *Exorcist III, Phantasm II, Friday the 13th Part 3,*

35

Die Hard 2: Die Harder, Scream 2, Halloween III: Season of the Witch and *Amityville II: The Possession*. Many will disagree with my choices and I'm cool with that. Not every sequel hit the mark, but those that did had a big impact.

A phenomenon that always fascinated me in the video era was that of the straight-to-video sequel. These were often riffing on something that had been popular on the big screen or something that had at least been a moderate hit on home video. Many of these sequels would try to bring back at least part of the main cast of the original, whereas the ones that were particularly strapped for cash would just cast Eric Roberts, because hey, he's a great bad guy. One thing is for certain - one thing the vast majority of straight-to-video sequels had in common was a desire to make some money off the back of a known property, because when you have brand familiarity, you can skimp on originality. That's not to say that straight-to-video sequels were universally bad - they could often take a few more chances than their more popular counterparts as there was less money at stake that needed to be made back.

Not many people now would be aware that there were two sequels to *From Dusk Til Dawn* for example, or that *The Crow* hit four movies before vanishing (I like to pretend the remake doesn't exist). Mind you, after *The Crow: Wicked Prayer* with Edward Furlong, David Bioreanaz and Tara Reid, it was best laid to rest.

The best example of straight-to-video fodder that went its own weird way would be the case of the forgotten sequels to sci-fi actioner *Universal Soldier*.

Long before Van Damme and Lundgren came back to the franchise, there were two TV movie sequels in the shape of

Universal Soldier II: Brothers in Arms (1998) and *Universal Soldier III: Unfinished Business* (also 1998). Those found their way to the UK market on VHS to a tepid - and I would imagine slightly confused - response. The lead in those films was a character called Luc Deveraux, played by Matt Battaglia, who had previously shown up as a bodyguard in the notoriously bad movie disasterpiece *Showgirls*. These TV movies also featured straight-to-video legend Jeff Wincott along with Gary Busey in II and Burt Reynolds in III, offering a very 'wtf' sort of experience for fans of the original movie.

As dodgy and low-rent as they may be, straight-to-video sequels had a charm of their own, and still get made even now, although it's a case of 'straight to streaming' or 'straight to cheap supermarket DVD' now. They were a great way for studios to wring a bit more cash from IPs they owned, but they also offered something new for fans and thus I would argue that they did have some merit. Here and now though, cheap sequels to existing franchises come in for a lot of abuse from critics (both professional and armchair) as in the age of giant 4K TVs, Blu-ray and HD streaming, the shortcomings and limitations of a production are painfully visible.

They seem more derided now in this more cynical age, but I remember straight-to-video sequels being a fun thing to watch. As much as I may take the piss out of the *Children of the Corn* and *Amityville* sequels, I admit I rented them and probably enjoyed them for their duration, as bad as they often were. Then there were franchise sequels I was always eager to see hit video shop shelves, such as the *Trancers* and *Puppet Master* series.

Straight-to-video sequels of the VHS era were able to take more risks than their big-budget counterparts, such as experimenting with storylines, different approaches to characters and even killing off cast members (I mean characters, not the actors themselves, of course).

Now with streaming services creating their own franchises with their own sequels, some movies that would have gone straight to video are now able to look much better and have better casts at their disposal, but these are limited to those projects with proper finance behind them from those streaming companies themselves. This leaves the cheaper stuff still looking, well, cheaper.

Has the advent of better technology democratised film production and allowed independent creators to make movies that stand shoulder to shoulder with bigger, richer productions? No, not really. They're still often visibly low-budget productions, but the advent and growth of streaming has made it easier for independent creators to get their films seen on the same platforms.

This is really evident on Amazon Prime, for example. I have gone down the Prime rabbit hole many times, finding endless weird and wonderful indie flicks that would never have found their way to mass distribution back in the day. Be it sci-fi, horror or action, every film I find seems to bring up suggestions for a dozen more that I've never heard of, and while many are trash, there is always a gem to be found.

Chapter Four
Franchises almost killed by their sequels

As much as I love sequels, it has to be said that they don't always enrich the lore of their franchises very well. Let's take a look at one of the most obvious examples of this to start with: *Freddy's Dead: The Final Nightmare.*

Released in 1991, this sixth entry in the series of *A Nightmare on Elm Street* movies was supposed to be the epic sendoff for Robert Englund's titular dream demon. The franchise had clearly run its course, considering the lukewarm reception to the previous film, *A Nightmare on Elm Street 5: The Dream Child*, so it made sense (I'm sure it did to someone) to give the story a final outing and kill Freddy off for once and all and squeeze some more cash out of fans aching for a new, better Freddy flick. There was a buzz around the horror magazines at the time that this final film would reclaim some of Krueger's grim glory and lay him to rest in style.

Sadly, the product that was spat out at us felt like a far lesser entry than even the much-maligned *Dream Child*. It was dreadful almost to the point of parody. To compare *Freddy's Dead: The Final Nightmare* to entries like the glory of *A Nightmare on Elm Street Part 3; Dream Warriors*, or indeed any of the previous pieces of the franchise, really shows how far the quality had slipped by this point.

The film is packed with cheap gimmicks, cameos (including the risible Roseanne Barr and an awkward Alice Cooper as Freddy's abusive father), effects that had aged even by the time the film came out, a terrible script with unlikeable characters and a beyond shoddy ending.

So. That ending. Spoiler alert if you want to wade through it at some point.

The film had a woeful 3D element which was clumsily integrated into the script. When the characters on screen donned 3D glasses, that was the audience's cue to put theirs on too. These glasses were handed out in cinemas as well as supplied with VHS copies of the film once it hit video. The gimmick certainly raised some interest from audiences eager to see Freddy get his last comeuppance in glorious 3D. It sounded amazing to me... until I saw it.

I was around 13 years old when it came out, and while I was deep into my horror obsession by this time (thanks to parents who were ok with me watching horror movies as I knew how the effects were done, thus taking away any fear of them), I couldn't see it at the cinema. I saw this as rather unfair as I was Freddy fixated at the time. I had the VHS tapes of the films, several tapes of the TV series spinoff *Freddy's Nightmares*, the books, the posters and even a plastic replica of his notorious glove. I'd even gone as far as writing some 'Young Freddy' stories starring a kid version of the dream demon, an act that I'd also done during my phase obsessing over ninjas, which gave rise to stories under the umbrella title of *The Young Ninja*.

(As an aside, while Freddy has never popped up in my writing career as an adult aside from writing about the films, my ninja character eventually came back into my life by inspiring the Violet Shadow character I created for AC Comics, appearing in some Femforce stories I wrote for them

as well as her own shorts that were eventually compiled into the Violet Shadow one-shot comic book they put out.)

After what seemed like an eternal wait I did get to see it on VHS from the video shop, including 3D glasses that were given with early rentals of it. I set up a perfect video night of snacks and drinks and sat down to soak in the final chapter of the Krueger saga.

Dear Reader, what I saw was *not* the epic finale that fans had been promised.

It carried no characters from earlier films, had a script that felt like it had been written with someone's arse cheeks, some painful dream sequences and an ending that was a long, long way from satisfying. In its defence, some of the direction from Rachel Talalay was pretty good, and her work has been something I've long since been fond of. This wasn't a high point. I sort of liked the idea of - SPOILER ALERT - Freddy being pulled into the real world and being blown up, but the effects used to achieve this shot - and the subsequent escaping dream demon wraiths - were atrocious. I mean, I love Troma and Full Moon, and even *their* effects walked all over this painful sequence.

The film killed Freddy, but it also killed the franchise for a while. It would be three years before the next film, *Wes Craven's New Nightmare*, would come along and give the series an epilogue which was ingenious and satisfying. I'll talk about that one later.

Freddy was far from being unique in his franchise being butchered by terrible sequels. The other horror icons of the 80s saw their franchises collapse under the sheer crapness of their later entries.

Jason Voorhees, with his iconic hockey mask (that didn't show up until the 3rd movie, trivia fans) and machete, managed to make it through seven movies before his franchise collapsed with the risible *Friday the 13th Part VIII: Jason Takes Manhattan* in 1989. While some fans enjoy its kitsch atmosphere and neon-lit visuals, it was a woeful attempt at bringing Jason to a new setting and beyond moving the location offered very little of interest. A further film arrived in 1993 in the form of *Jason Goes to Hell: The Final Friday*, which brought a new supernatural aspect to the series and, while better than Part VIII, killed the franchise for years to come. *The Final Friday* ended with the brilliant shot of Jason's mask being dragged into the underworld by Freddy Krueger's razor glove, but the promise of the eventual *Freddy Vs Jason* film wasn't fulfilled until 2003. By that time, Jason had already returned for the supremely silly but rather entertaining *Jason X*, in which we saw Jason in space, being turned into a cyborg. There was a *Friday the 13th* remake a few years later but as with many remakes, it sucked all the life and promise out of the franchise once again, effectively killing Jason once and for all.

The *Hellraiser* series was another that started strong with the original indie *Hellraiser* movie in 1987 and the baroque, epic horror of *Hellbound: Hellraiser II* in 1988. In 1993 the third entry, *Hellraiser III: Hell On Earth* arrived, and pretty much destroyed the goodwill of the first two films with a quip-laden misfire. The series continued nonetheless with increasingly lower returns. *Hellraiser IV: Bloodline* was a valiant attempt at telling a story that crossed generations of the bloodline that created the Lament Configuration puzzle

43

box in the first place, but didn't have the power to rebuild what part 3 had destroyed. The series then went straight to video/DVD with the sequels *Inferno, Hellseeker, Deader* and *Hellworld*. Pinhead himself, Doug Bradley, would then jump ship before the tiny-budget sequels *Revelations* and *Judgement* were made. Eventually, a new *Hellraiser* would arrive on streaming services, but to only a middling response from audiences.

The Texas Chainsaw Massacre wasn't immune to crappy sequels, either. The original is a masterpiece of tension, panic and not actually showing much gore. *The Texas Chainsaw Massacre 2* was a crazy fever dream and *Leatherface: Texas Chainsaw Massacre 3* was a mess, but nowhere near the franchise killer that was *Texas Chainsaw Massacre: The Next Generation* in 1996. It may have had some decent talent in it in the form of Matthew McConaughey and Renee Zellweger among the cast, but even their skills were lost in a mire of self-referential fluff. The franchise was dead until the 2003 remake, the remake's prequel and a further reimagining were all churned out to little effect.

Wes Craven's *The Hills Have Eyes* (1977) had a notoriously dreadful sequel arrive in 1984 with *The Hills Have Eyes Part 2*. Again directed by Craven, this rush-job of a film stars a cast of sub-*Friday the 13th* teenagers who are part of a motorbike sports club, fighting off the cannibalistic advances of what remains of the first film's family of mutants. Apparently, only two-thirds of the film were shot before the budget ran out and Craven had to pad the sequel out with flashbacks from the first film. While this took the movie up to feature length, it just serves to highlight how

44

lacking the new characters and story are, resulting in a disjointed flick that leaves you with the same empty feeling as a disappointing fast food meal. The franchise wouldn't return until a remake arrived in 2006 and a sequel to the remake (which was way, way better than the 1984 sequel) in 2007. That 2007 version of *The Hills Have Eyes 2* introduced a group of National Guard trainees, making the battle against the mutants way more interesting - and way more violent. I do recommend that one.

The list goes on. *Halloween, Batman, Terminator, Robocop, Jaws, Alien*, so many franchises were damaged badly by their own sequels. What interests me about this trend is that so many are big-screen franchises rather than low-budget series. It seems to be the case that many low-budget franchises (such as Full Moon's aforementioned *Puppet Master*) can keep on pumping out sequels and manage to keep going regardless of the numbers they bring in. There seems to be a loyalty to those low-budget gems that the big names just can't maintain.

In the VHS era, it seemed to be the case that, whatever the apparent quality of the product, if it had a sequel number slapped onto it then it would get rentals. There would often be multiple copies - the surefire sign that a shop had faith in a title. That could backfire sometimes as the brand familiarity of franchises like *Children of the Corn* or *Amityville* and the relatively low budgets needed to make flicks for them resulted in video stores being flooded with increasingly rubbish products that ultimately faded away until remakes started being vomited out at an alarming rate.

The lesser sequels to beloved (and not-so-beloved) franchises are still fun to collect on tape as they satisfy that completist streak many of us have. I mean, it's damn satisfying to see all of them on the shelf together.

That satisfaction is often a better feeling than actually watching some of those things. I mean, I may sniff at *Freddy's Dead,* but it's still better than *Children of the Corn III: Urban Harvest* with the monster-grabbing action figures that were supposed to be people!

There are some gems to be found in the world of straight-to-video sequels, however, whatever you do, don't ever, ever watch the two sequels to *The Lost Boys.*

Consider that advice a public service.

VIDEO VARIETY
MYSTERY
TAPES!
£1 each

Interlude: It's tape time on YouTube

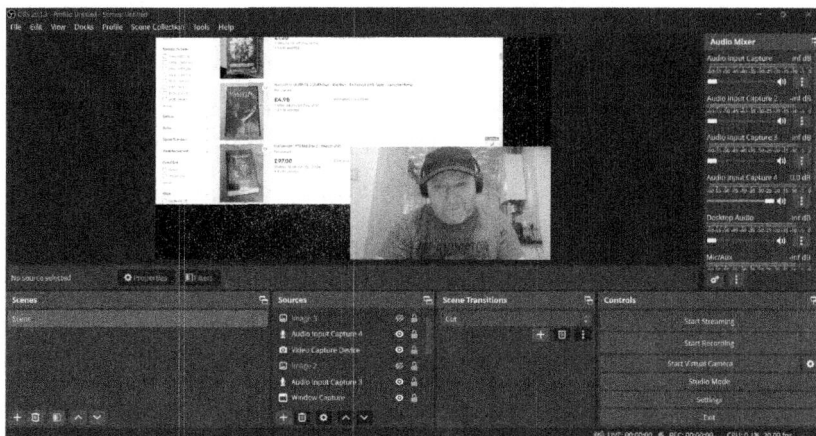

I look through the settings in OBS Studio, again ignoring the reminder to update to a newer version. I like this one. I make sure the camera is as clear as it can be (which isn't perfect but hey, I'm not monetised yet. I have to make do with what I've got). I make sure the ring light isn't washing me out completely. I check the mic levels. They can vary depending on what I'm using. If I use the studio mic I need to remember to stay pretty still. If I clip on my lapel mic then it can start going into the red. If it's the headset I have a bit more freedom, even though it makes me look like I'm back in my call centre days.

Next, I check if I've got the right tabs open and they display okay in the Window Capture channel in OBS. I've taken to having things open in tabs rather than flicking between things in OBS or editing in later as it's easier to manage and reduces the length of my edit sessions.

48

My available time for content creation is limited, often sandwiched between everyone else going to bed and me following them. That's why most of my content is shot at night - it's the only free time I really have to dedicate to a hobby (it's also when this book was written - much like the original - through many late nights). Family life, a full-time job and the myriad stresses of modern life are not that conducive to creating quality stuff.

The golden rule for YouTube videos is 'aim for ten minutes', but I usually aim for twenty. I figure that the majority of my audience is a bit more mature and has longer attention spans. I've tried various lengths over the history of my channel and twenty minutes works best for me, allowing for an intro, the main topic, some tangents and my often-fumbled outros.

I check the notes I've made for tonight's recording of Planet Hex. I've got a running order of things I want to cover. I need to remember to take up less time with the intro to the video and get to the meat of it as intros have been too long in recent videos. Then again, do my subscribers enjoy the parts where I'm just chatting? I do get a lot of comments about the tangents I go off on and the bits of trivia I pepper each episode with.

Am I making the content for myself or my viewers? I'm not sure. Mainly I just want to nerd out over things that scratch the nostalgia itch for me or share some knowledge about obscure films or cartoons or action figures or whatever. The VHS-themed videos are the ones I enjoy making the most. No surprises there.

Why carry on making these things? I don't have tons of subscribers or a big reach or anything. I don't earn anything from the videos. I don't have thousands of comments under episodes or anything like that. I don't care really. When I wrote the original version of *VHS Ate My Brain,* I did it because I wanted to give something back to the niche scene that had become so important to me. That's what I'm doing on YouTube, or when I guest on other channels or podcasts. I'm being part of it all in my little way. I want to join in with those people dotted around the world who still get a thrill from the sound of a clamshell case popping open or the sound of a tape spooling up in a player.

I start recording, take a breath, raise a hand in greeting to the camera and grin. "Hey, welcome to Planet Hex. I'm Andrew Hawnt."

I feel great. I feel included and enthusiastic. I spend twenty minutes sharing that enthusiasm and I can't wait to post it. I start editing.

No wonder the nights are long.

Chapter Five
Why do I still love this stuff?

I've sat down to watch *Terror Vision* (1986) after not seeing it for many years. I picked it up from eBay recently, which was chronicled on my YouTube channel as all of my tape hunts on there are at the moment. I love this flick. Produced by Charles Band and released by Empire Pictures way before their collapse and eventual rebirth as Full Moon Entertainment (now known as Full Moon Features), it holds a special place for me for a few reasons.

First I'm a big fan of Charles Band, Empire Pictures and Full Moon due to their sheer audacity and the attitude of their films. During the golden period of Full Moon, it seemed like there was always a *Trancers*, a *Demonic Toys* or a *Puppet Master* film from them I hadn't watched yet when I would visit the video store. They tend to be ridiculous in the best way, with a comic book atmosphere and tongues planted firmly in cheek.

This one has the added bonus for me of being laced with 80s heavy metal references, which is an instant mark of quality for me as an increasingly frazzled old metalhead. It's a fun watch. There are dumb jokes, wobbly sets, cheap effects and questionable performances, but I love it. I love it for all of those reasons, all of those things that audiences now would see as hackneyed or even downright unwatchable. That's the thing that sets tapeheads apart from normal film fans I'd say.

The ability to enjoy something for what it is, despite its obvious limitations, is something VHS fans have honed over a lifetime. Basically, we'll sit through any old crap and find something about it we like or at least something of note. I don't think this is because we're connoisseurs of underground cinema or anything as pompous as that. I just think our tolerance for trash is way higher than others.

So why do things like *Terror Vision* still fill me with such unabashed, unironic joy? I think, maybe, that I have always felt like I was in on the joke, Yes, I know that these things were cheap, rushed and a million

52

miles away from being seen as high art, but I always got the feeling that the filmmakers made them for idiots like me and our knowing smirks. Yeah, we get it, we know this is trash, but we're having a ton of fun nonetheless.

It was often a case of looking at the company that put a tape out that would tell me if I was going to like it or not. When I'd see names like Full Moon Entertainment, Empire Pictures, Medusa Home Video, VipCo or Palace, I knew I'd get my money's worth.

I have always revelled in the weird, the kitsch, the gory and the unsettling, along with a healthy dose of the silly, the obscure and the far-fetched.

One of my earliest memories of falling in love with horror and genre films was *GoreZone* issue 17 in the early 90s. Bought from my regular haunt the Sheffield Space Centre, it blew my mind with its graphic content and its coverage of weird and wonderful films. What caught me about that was the how-to guide on the methods used in applying the *Darkman* makeup to Liam Neeson in the film of the same name, which was directed with typical flair by Sam Raimi.

That guide went through each step of the process, from the application of a bald wig over Neeson's hair through to the finished product. Let's see if I remember. It was seven pieces in total aside from the bald cap, and each was shown in the moulds that kept the latex in shape. As each one was applied there was less of Neeson (or at least the model or dummy that was used for the process) visible and more of Darkman taking his place. At the end of it, there was the star of the movie in all of his grim, skinless and burned glory. The latex, glue and paint had worked their magic.

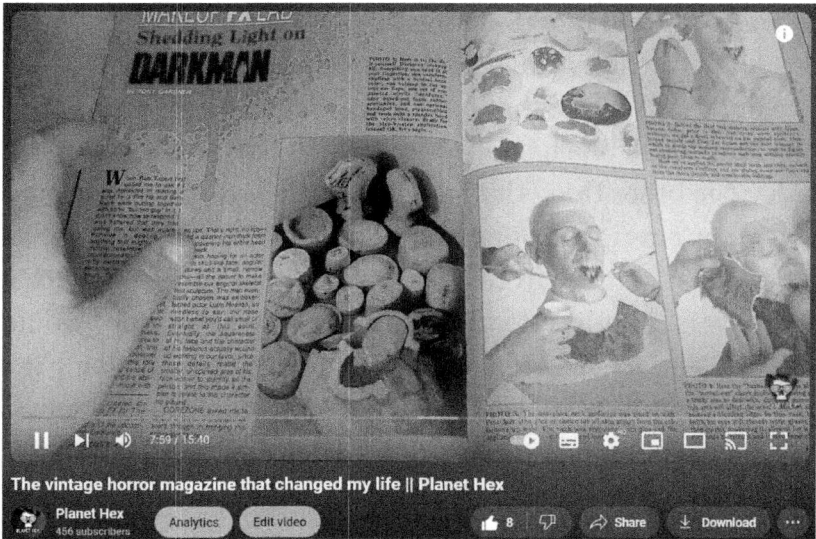

I immediately became fascinated by horror makeup and, fuelled by the book *The Making of Ghostbusters*, my fascination extended to scripts, lighting, direction, soundtracks and more. Films of every level of quality became incredible experiences for me. Rather than just getting 90 minutes of entertainment, I would go over them again and examine the effects sequences, picking out what was makeup, what was animatronic or what was camera tricks.

That addiction to how genre movies are made has continued to this day, and I'm so grateful that my understanding of how things are made still hasn't got in the way of me enjoying most things. At heart I'm still the same kid who was watching horror movies I was far too young for, only now I'm a bald guy in my forties watching that same era of cinematic cheese.

Am I a bad movie apologist? No, I can happily say that a lot of the films I love from the VHS era are complete junk, but they're junk that people worked to produce, no matter how much of a barrel-scraping exercise they turn out to be.

The other thing that keeps me watching movies from other eras is the opportunity to delve into times it's easy to view as simpler from our vantage point of the future. Life now is chaotic, relentless and unpredictable, but I would argue that each era feels like that to the people living it because each era has become more complicated than what preceded it.

Nostalgia, to me, is the act of indulging in things from an era that strike a familiar chord. For cult film fans I would argue that chord rings out through eras earlier than the one we have lived through. While my main loves are 80s and 90s movies, I can equally lose myself in flicks from any decade back to the 1930s.

Those are more alien to me, but the slower pace of life and the lack of things that are so very prevalent in the modern era (such as smartphones and the omnipresence of the internet in every facet of our lives) is refreshing. It's like taking a brief holiday from being bombarded with notifications from emails, social media, your family, your groups, your damn streaming services and everything else that is vying for our attention now.

I look at old movies and see myself in situations like those on the screen. I remember being a kid reading comics in my bedroom while listening to cassettes or the radio, then putting on a video. Yes, that makes me sound increasingly like a grumpy old man, but I remember what the experience was like of life without the ever-present danger of someone calling you for a video chat, piping up on a voice channel in a video game or demanding that you like, share and subscribe.

So nostalgia is the main driving force in me still loving these things, but it's not the whole story. I still love these things because many of them still really entertain me for the stories and performances. Old 80s sword and sorcery movies still pull me into them wholeheartedly with their physical effects and sincere performances. I'm not constantly distracted by thinking "Ooh, cool CGI. That CGI building blew up well. Oh look, the CGI monster is rendered really beautifully. Oh, CGI space battle. Yikes, that CGI de-aging looks off."

I mean, after you realise that, you start seeing the characters as the actors playing them rather than the characters in the story. Big event movies are terrible for this of late. I'm looking at you, Marvel Studios and the clowns behind the DC movies. They end up looking like cutscenes from video games, even more so since games technology continues to race ahead of other forms of media.

Do I have a vendetta against modern films? Not really. Most aren't to my taste, but I do love modern cinema as well. It's just that my heart is in a clamshell VHS box. I mean, not really as that would be weird, but you get what I mean. I was raised with video stores in all of their grimy glory before Blockbuster came along and sucked the life out of the video market with the oversaturation of mediocre and sanitized products, leaving out interesting smaller films completely.

VHS tapes may be filled with a lot of junk among the classics, but I still love them. They happened, and they were hugely influential to lives across the planet for many years. Not just for films, but in homes, in schools, hospitals, businesses, official buildings and way more. Heck, all the way down to watching pirate tapes of stuff on coach trips (I did that a few times, but it was usually shit like *Coronation Street* rather than anything good. I mean, bloody hell, I would have settled for crap like *Police Academy* over *Coronation Street*. Anything but that maudlin phlegm splat of a soap.

I don't want VHS tapes to be forgotten. They should be celebrated. I doubt many of them will ever be seen as great works of art, but the effect they had on the development of popular culture and our social awareness can't be denied.

Chapter Six
The Death of Hunting in the Wild

I'm calling it. Tape hunting in the wild is stone dead. Its rotting corpse is festering in a skip somewhere, buried under audio cassettes, old radio alarm clocks and mouldy cookbooks. With pretty much all charity shops no longer accepting donations of VHS tapes, they have all but vanished from the hunting grounds that were once so fertile.

I've talked about the slow decline of hunting tapes in the wild before in print and on YouTube, with fewer and fewer places still carrying tapes, but now as far as I can see, the scene is dead in the wild.

That's not to say that tapes aren't still out there somewhere, but they certainly aren't in the cities and shops I've visited these past few years. Only one charity shop near our house still carries tapes, and they only have a few Disney titles and a couple of sports things, as I guess those are the ones they see as collectable. They have my details in case any ex-rentals come in (and not just horror - at this point, I'd be amazed to see any genre at all show up locally), but I'm not holding my breath.

Tapes are now almost solely found through other collectors, be it on eBay or through the myriad retro-themed social media accounts that have blossomed throughout the scene in recent years. A few speciality shops I know of carry tapes, and that's really cool, but the chance of coming across them by accident in a far-flung charity shop is zero right now. I knew this would happen as there's always been a finite number of the things out there, but the death of tape hunting in the wild (at least in vast chunks of the UK) has made me ask a question.

Is it my fault?

Did the original *VHS Ate My Brain* plus the videos, podcasts and magazine columns I did contribute to VHS being snapped up for bargain prices? Did my work, and that of others like me on YouTube and in print, directly contribute to tapes vanishing from sight? Or was it a combination of the above and the fact that they are an obsolete format that was left in the dust by discs and - more recently - streaming and as such seen as junk that nobody wants? They were seen as pretty much junk back when I did the first *VHS Ate My Brain*, so ten years later that can only have been reinforced.

The collector market has boomed in the past decade, with individual films and studios and stars being the focus of a great many collectors new to the hobby. Perhaps we, the collectors and content creators who were there in the scene's formative days, are to blame for the rise in prices and the lack of tapes in the public eye.

Or am I reading too much into our limited influence? The big money tapes were already circulating on the collector market way before it became hard to find stuff in the wild. Labels of choice were already bringing in a pretty penny, so has the vast amount of VHS-themed content that has come up in recent years contributed that much?

Personally, I think it has. By showing the world our love for the format and the films it carried, I believe that we have created the market as it is today. This has been further bolstered by the occasional clickbait-style story in the mainstream media about tapes selling for thousands. Suddenly instead of bunging them in landfill or into charity shops, tapes find their way onto eBay with inflated prices that gradually force the prices of other tapes up, artificially inflating what each one may be worth.

I may be overthinking this, or I may just be salty that the tapes I want have become out of my price range. But while tapes have become almost impossible to find in the wild, what isn't hard to find these days is like-minded fans, and personally that may be even better than finding a tape here or there. If the past decade has taught me anything, it's that I could find my tribe. It had to happen eventually, and getting to occasionally spend time around people who understand and share my love for this stuff is absolute gold.

I put a video out on my YouTube channel in which I ask if hunting in the wild is dead and I asked for comments from viewers as to what hunting is like where they are. Comments were divided between a few people who agreed that hunting in the wild was dead, while a few others commented that tapes still show up around them from time to time. Those, unsurprisingly, were in America.

Why do they still show up more over there? Perhaps because there are more out-of-the-way towns and cool flea markets and weird collectable places in the States. Simple as that. And thrift stores seem to still have a few when I see them online as well. I'm a big fan of many YouTube channels that feature an element of retro hunting. Retro Rick and Ed's Retro Geek Out are a couple of particular favourites. They often come across tapes in the world on their travels, and while VHS isn't the focus of their content (Rick is more about video games and toys while Ed is mostly vintage toys), they do tend to note when places have tapes available. Looking at those places through the lens of a guy thousands of miles away is weird. Many of the cool places they visit seem stuffed to the gills with tapes, laserdiscs, audio cassettes and other vintage goodies, while over here in the charity shops pretty much all you usually see right now are dog-eared cookbooks, jigsaws and millions of paperbacks.

The nostalgia for VHS runs deep for me, right back to very early childhood memories, but now a second layer of nostalgia has taken hold. I miss the scene of ten years ago. There have been some brilliant things happening in the scene in that time, with acceptance and awareness of it achieving greater heights than I thought possible, but with that wider appeal and awareness has come the loss of the hunt.

I'm missing the adventures I wrote about then. The weird little shops like the one I found with action figures nailed to a board like in the lair of a psychopath, the one with the massive stacks of pornography, the furniture shop with a family in it that watched my every move as I examined their wall of ex-rentals. They're all gone.

One place that remains is the corner shop where I found over thirty tapes on one magical day. They had sold me all of them for 50p each. It was my greatest haul of all time. The shop is still there. If you ever find yourself in Sherwood here in Nottingham, it's the little corner shop that now has a pharmacy in it as well. The cage of tapes is long gone, but around the back of the shop, you can still see the sign from one of their previous names- Sherwood Video. The sign is propped up with the bins and other stuff at the rear of the building, even more faded and weatherbeaten than it was the first time I saw it a decade ago.

Mind you, I too am more faded and weatherbeaten these days as well. Maybe I've lost the drive to go further and search harder, just because of the circumstances of having a family and working full time. Opportunities to go on a VHS road trip are few and far between now, so I am stuck with the notion that yes, hunting for tapes in the wild is dead.

This does mean that a lot of good stuff can now be found in specialist shops, but at much higher prices as they know what they have on their hands. I can't complain about that. They're charging what tapes are worth and they need to pay bills. I'm cool with that, but I'm not going to lie - I am in mourning for the joy of a fruitful hunt.

As such, my retro hunting these days has expanded to include books and music related to films I love, along with t-shirts and other memorabilia. Sometimes I will pick titles up on DVD if they're of interest, but it's not the same as finding a tape. Not for me.

Man, nostalgia is a funny thing.

Did I speak too soon?

Wait, what?

The day after I wrote the above paragraphs on how VHS hunting in the wild is dead, and less than twelve hours after I said there were barely any tapes around, I found some in not one, not two, but THREE charity shops all on the same street.

I hadn't slept well over the weekend. Such is the way with a brain that is fantastic at some things and terrible at others. Work had thus been quite a challenge for a couple of days, so I took a rare afternoon off. I wanted a bit of time out to myself. I didn't have time to go far, so that was the city centre out of the equation, so I opted instead for Sherwood. The plan would be a quick low-key retro hunt in Sherwood's wide range of charity shops (each with its own vibe), looking out for vintage comics, paperbacks and t-shirts, which was usually what I found there.

In one place I found two VHS tapes mixed in with the CDs and DVDs. Both musicals. Certainly not my scene, but it was cool to see them. In the next one, I found *three* tapes, all big blockbusters I again didn't have much interest in. But in the next, which I knew as a more 'vintage' themed charity shop (with a TARDIS-shaped changing room, no less), I came across a whole stack of tapes. Maybe twenty in total, mixed in with the basket of DVDs. I couldn't believe my eyes. There were films, mainly classics, mixed in with some concert tapes and sports and comedy, but they were tapes nonetheless. I went through the whole lot, and while I hadn't found anything for my shelves, I'd found VHS in the wild, properly, for what felt like the first time in years.

I went and asked the pleasant guy sorting shelves if they had any more VHS that weren't out on display.

"We haven't, I'm afraid. They're all out today. Whenever we get them in, they tend to sell really quickly."

I left smiling, reminded that tapeheads were still out there, still hunting, still not giving up.

I'll head back there soon, just in case.

After all, 'just in case' is what the hunt is all about.

I am starting to wonder if I was wrong about tapes never coming back, as had long since been my opinion, as more have started showing up. A regular haunt of mine started carrying a couple of crates of Disney tapes, which are of literally no interest to me but were cool to see. I checked back again and found some *Doctor Who* tapes featuring John Pertwee and Tom Baker's iteration of the ritual Time Lord. I bought those. The next time I went in I found a copy of *Prehysteria*, made under the Full Moon Features family film spinoff label Moonbeam. I bought that too. I didn't desperately want any of those, but I was excited in the moment by being able to buy VHS tapes locally again. I very much doubt it will grow beyond a few showing up here and there any time soon, but a vinyl-style resurgence may not be the pipe dream I had previously entertained.

Author's note: Tapes continue to show up in charity shops on an increasingly regular basis. I'm enjoying it while it lasts.

Interlude: Return of the Living Dead at the Savoy

It's been raining all day. I've done a full day's work, made everyone dinner and ran errands so I'm tired and cranky. I drive out in the rain, headlights on full, stressed that I can barely see the faded road markings thanks to the water and the clashing lights of other cars. After twenty minutes I'm where I need to be, or at least a few streets away once I'd found somewhere to park. I hurry through the bastard weather and turn the corner. That's when I see the cinema boards and the stress melts away, excitement taking its place.

Return of the Living Dead, 8:30pm, the backlit board declares. A film nerd (I can spot them by sight these days) is taking a photo of the board. He acknowledges me and I take out my phone to do the same, like two trainspotters on a platform, snapping away at a treasured engine.

ROTLD had been lined up for a cinema screening by the people behind The Loft Movie Theatre, a film club specialising in cult classics, along with my friend Rob Lane from the *Straight to Video* podcast and the 80s Video Shop in Alfreton. I buy what feels like a bucket of Pepsi Max and head up to screen 1, where I discover a crowd way bigger than I'd expected for a 1985 horror comedy showing on a night of vile weather.

The Loft gang and Rob do an intro with wireless mics. There's a giveaway (I decide not to join in, worrying it'd look like a fix if I won), then we settle in to watch a ludicrous - and ludicrously fun - film together.

The crowd laughs at the jokes and ridiculousness of it all, but it's not the laughter of derision. It's affectionate. The comedy beats hit home, and some of the more shonky special effects raise a giggle as well.

It's my first time seeing *ROTLD* on the big screen. Until now it's been the VHS copies I've owned or rented along with one DVD. Seeing it on the big screen makes me love it even more. The soundtrack is superb, the punk rock party atmosphere of it is infectious, and its pace winds tighter and tighter up to its apocalyptic climax. The credits roll and the crowd applauds and cheers. We all just rocked out in our seats to 90 minutes of gore, foul language, crude jokes and brain-eating, and we loved it.

We come out of the auditorium. I hang out with Rob briefly. I'm recognised by a reader of *VHS Ate My Brain* named Adam. We chat and fist bump. The crowd are all on a high. A chunk of the audience has just seen the film for the first time. I wonder what the heck they made of Linnea Quigley's infamous scene where her character dances naked on a grave. It's quite an eye-opener, as full-frontal nudity tends to be when viewed on a giant screen. I head out into the night. Thankfully the rain has stopped pouring, making my drive home way easier.

I drive home listening to the film's soundtrack at a ridiculous volume. It was beautiful to sit in the Savoy, not just watching a film I love, but being surrounded by a crowd of people who share my appreciation for these absurd old movies. I love being reminded that I'm not alone. There are a ton of cool people around the world who love these things too.

Tonight it was really heartening to spend time with some of them.

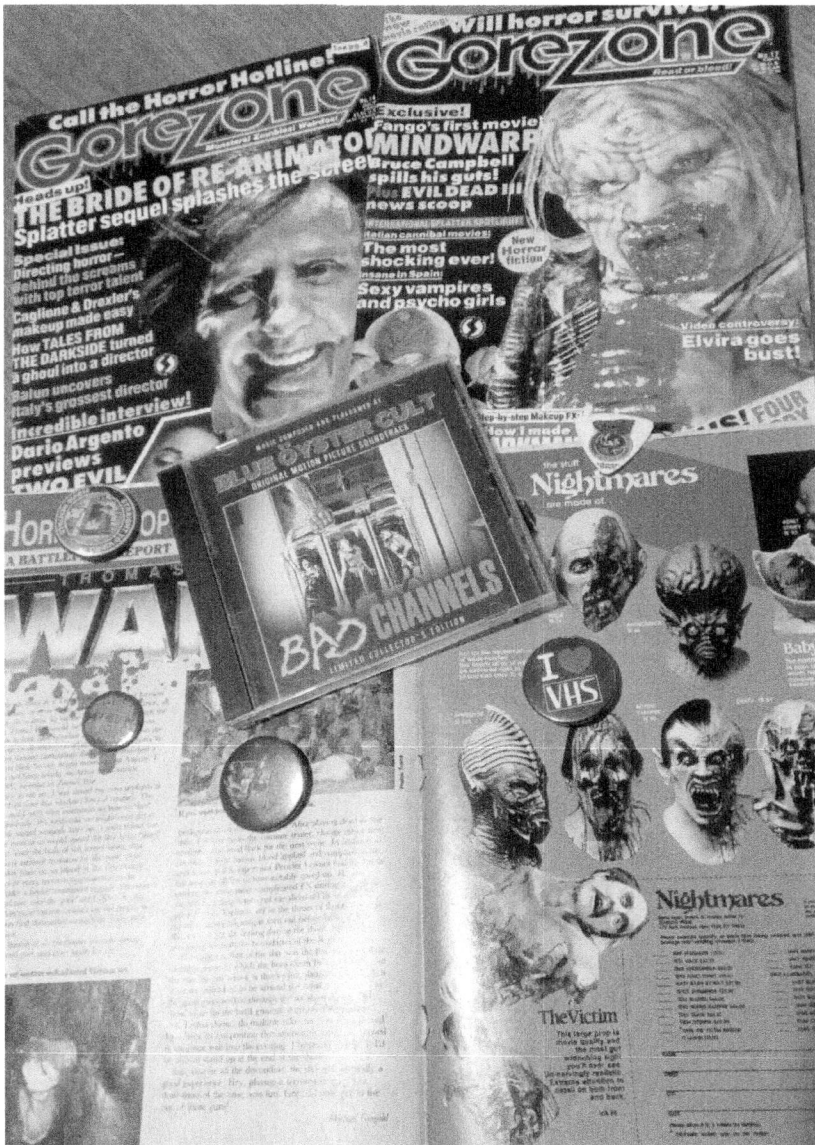

Chapter seven
The Cultural Shared Memory of Video Stores

I spent a lot of time in video stores, to the point where it was almost like going to church for me. I revered and respected the tapes, even if they housed *Ski School, Rawhead Rex and Police Academy 7: Mission to Moscow.* They had done their thing and been successful, or at least successful enough to warrant a video release.

The video store is burned into the hearts and minds of millions around the world. Just mentioning video stores takes many of us right back to nights spent choosing films, grabbing snacks and heading home for movie nights. Those movie night memories are probably accompanied by memories of old hairstyles, the layout of homes long since left behind and good times.

If you are too young to remember the feel, the smell and the atmosphere of video stores, I will do my best to give you an idea what they were like and why they continue to matter to people, not only years on from them vanishing, but a decade on from me getting nostalgic about them in print.

Video stores were more than just somewhere to rent flicks. I mean, that was their primary function, yes, but they had a lot more going for them than that. Those of us who remember them will speak of them like shrines, or the greatest meeting places, or somewhere you could lose yourself while you decided on that night's escapism.

Even the chains like Ritz or Blockbuster have a special place in many hearts, but it's the weird little independent shops, or 'Mom and pop' stores as our American friends refer to them, which garner the most love. Some were less than clean, some were in dodgy areas or operated by suspicious individuals, but whatever sort of state they were in, they had a magic about them. They were doorways to something cool. It was easy to get excited about the video store.

They would shape your media intake, right from the kid's sections with their cartoons and family titles right through to the extreme horror titles and that weird netherworld of the 'adult' section. The contents of a video store would traverse lifetimes. Whatever age you were, whatever your interests and preferences, the local video store had your back.

The fact that so many people used video stores for such a long time, say from the early eighties to the mid-2000s, is a clear explanation of why they have entered into the pantheon of things that immediately evoke a time, a place and a situation when they are mentioned.

Of course, as technology moved on and the humble VCR was superseded by the DVD player, Blu-Ray and the internet, stores thinned out and eventually vanished, leaving just the warm glow of nostalgia behind.

Video rental stores offered a cheaper alternative to buying films outright - you could pick them up for a weekend for a small price and have fun, then drop them back at the store and get your next fix. They avoided cluttering houses with film libraries and your favourite titles were there waiting for you time and again until the tapes broke or were sold by the stores. They didn't vanish from stores like films and shows do now on streaming services. Well, not unless someone didn't return the tape, but then they would be burned at the stake for their crimes. Well, not quite that, but they should have been.

I was among the crowd that saw visiting the video store as an event in itself. I have waxed lyrical on many occasions about the hours I would spend in Metro Video, deciding on the right double - or triple-bill for the night before getting snacks and drinks and picking up posters and whatnot that they had put aside for me. I loved being there. I wanted to work there. The video store staff were my heroes and they never knew. I never told them what they meant to me, and

71

by the time it had occurred to me to do so, they were gone, left behind by popular culture's addiction to the next thing.

I'm proud to be a relic of the video store era. I loved those places and the tatty covers on tapes and the background music and the little TVs showing promo tapes of trailers and the wall of rental tapes visible behind the counter, all of them sat on their sides to show the code that matched the stickers they had applied to the sleeves.

If you ask film fanatics what they remember about being at the video store, many will mention the gaudy cover art. The rows of films were all fighting for attention, and it was often the case that the lower budget and niche movies, especially horror movies and science fiction, would have outrageous cover art that ended up creating a crazy mosaic of images on the shelves that have been burned into the minds of those who visited. Cheap titles sat alongside classics and big-budget blockbusters, but all were equal on those shelves.

Yes, video stores were often chaotic and a little overwhelming, but their limited stock made choosing films way easier than getting caught in an endless loop of flicking through 'content' on streaming services. The stock in these stores wasn't just a commodity, it was a carefully curated and assembled library that was intended to appeal to as wide an audience as possible, created by people rather than algorithms.

When video stores went the way of the dinosaurs, we saw a cultural shift in real-time. Viewers were trying out the new technologies, and I get that. It was exciting to enjoy something that didn't need the tracking changing in order to work.

But now we see nostalgia for times when our viewing wasn't observed by the companies we pay subscription fees to. A time when we were free to check out a bunch of films without having similar titles rammed down our throats, sometimes as soon as the credits rolled on what we'd just finished.

The lasting muscle memory of video rental stores reminds us of community, formative years and times that were less chaotic. You know, times that were rather more analogue.

A brilliant example of how that shared memory of video stores can spark emotion, nostalgia and a longing for different times can be found in the documentary *The Last Blockbuster*. That 2020 film, directed by Taylor Morden, is an affectionate, funny and often poignant examination of life at the last functional branch of Blockbuster in the world. Through the eyes of the staff and the customers that still frequent the place, we see firsthand the movement between ages of consumerism, from the physical and tangible to the digital and vague. We see a place that is the livelihood of several people and that has served a community for a long, long time. We see people who have grown up with the video store nearby and who know its every inch. We see props there and memorabilia from films that are turning the place itself into a sort of living museum. We see the struggles of maintaining a business in the face of the entire industry it serves being replaced by digital content you don't need to leave the house for.

At its heart, it's about the people running it, which is what would make or break a good video store. The people running it needed to know their stuff. They needed to encourage customers to check other titles out that they may enjoy. They were the custodians of everybody's entertainment for a damn long time and had the knowledge and the heart that no algorithm will ever be able to replace.

The video stores I have visited over the years were their own beasts. Even the chain video stores like Video Magic in my early days, then onto Ritz and Blockbuster, each branch had its own vibe, be it the decor, the layout or the stock they carried.

But of course, nothing to me will ever compare to the joy and - weirdly - safety I felt while in Metro Video in Sheffield. It was its own entity, full of big ideas and cheap movies, snacks and posters and standees and chaos.

No wonder I could relate to it.

The shared muscle memory of hanging out in video stores is a chapter in the shared experience of several generations. They weren't for an age bracket or really any specific demographic. They were for all of us. They were one of the only genuinely cross-generational and cross-background forms of entertainment that has ever excited the masses, and I can't imagine that in years to come there will be people reminiscing about flicking through streaming services for hours on end.

As so many VHS-era stories include the things that went on around going to the video shop, be it nights in, meals, time with family and friends that may no longer be with us, going and getting a video out was a tribal act that lasted far longer than many other forms of entertainment.

Video shops, I salute you.

Chapter Eight
Ten years of retro culture

A lot has happened in the appreciation of VHS, and indeed physical media as a whole, since I first thought "Hey, I'll write something about VHS. Nobody will read it but it'd be fun."

The biggest cultural explosion in awareness of retro media and aesthetics began in 2016 with the explosion in popularity of the Netflix hit *Stranger Things*, but I'll be talking about that in the next chapter. This one will talk about the media's coverage of VHS and related things like video stores over the past decade, and how our niche appreciation of a bygone platform has turned out to not be quite as niche as we thought.

Just one month after *VHS Ate My Brain* popped up for sale in 2014, a man in Idaho came to the attention of the media when USA Today and other outlets picked up the story that he had made it his mission to collect every VHS copy of *Speed* ever produced. Fair play, but wouldn't it have been a better service to the world to grab all copies of *Speed 2: Cruise Control* to ensure that it never darkened a player ever again?

The Guardian took a look at pages from an old Argos catalogue and noted that a quality VHS recorder would set you back £599. What would £599 get you in 2024? Well, more to the point, who HAS £599 in 2024?

Nintendo Life covered the story of a NES (Nintendo Entertainment System) fan who had built a fully functional console inside a VHS tape. You have to admit it doesn't get much more 80s than a VHS tape you can play *Super Mario Bros* on.

In October 2014 *The Guardian* touched on VHS again when it reported about 20th Century Flicks, a video store in Bristol that was still defiantly open. Naturally, as with many instances where the media finds enthusiasts about anything, the piece came across a bit derisory, or maybe that's just me being a bitter old man. I just checked and from what I can see, 20th Century Flicks is still in business, rocking a screening room, store and rental service. That absolutely rules.

March 2015 saw a university library in New Haven, US, acquired 2,700 VHS tapes (mainly horror and exploitation movies) from a collector called Joe Pesch. I wish I could have had a rummage through those!

That April, a French artist known as Golem13 unveiled a series of VHS covers made for modern movies as an art project, creating retro covers for films like *Guardians of the Galaxy, Interstellar* and *Gravity* and TV shows like *Game of Thrones* and *Breaking Bad*, among others.

The Guardian were at it again in July, filling a slow news day with an appreciation of VHS cover art, while *C-Ville* reported on the sad closure of Sneak Previews, a long-running video store in Charlottesville. Many of his tapes, like Mr Pesch earlier, would be donated to universities. I bet university movie nights kicked ass.

Then there was a rather more poignant story about how an archive of VHS tapes shot between 1982-1992 became the basis of a groundbreaking documentary about Bosnian refugees entitled *Flotel Europa*. This demonstrates my long-standing belief that VHS tapes are historical artefacts and the first real example of history being captured exactly as it happened.

2015 also saw a VHS aesthetic iPhone app hitting the headlines after becoming a massive hit, and apps of its type are still to be found today.

In November 2015 came the announcement that Sony would discontinue production of Betamax tapes after 40 years, and almost three decades since VHS overtook it in popularity. What an odd thought, that even in 2015 there were still Betamax tapes being made somewhere. Who the heck was buying them?

This brings me to the hellscape that was 2016. David Bowie died only 10 days into the year. No doubt when David went back to his home planet it set off a series of mad events that played out like the prologue to a post-apocalyptic film. A referendum about something or other happened and made a gigantic mess here in the UK. Overseas in the US, an orange man became president. Whichever side of the fence you dwell, it was a really weird year.

2016 also saw the debut of the aforementioned *Stranger Things,* which we'll get to.

That aside, the big event of 2016 for VHS came in the early Summer, when Funai Electronics, the last company apparently still making VCRs, ended production of them. My backup player is a Funai, which had been passed to me by my mother as she hadn't used it once. This came after my original JVC died after 25 years of use. The Funai is a great player, but knowing it was one of the last is an odd and slightly poignant thing. A reminder that the world has moved on since the days of all this stuff that excited me. The video shops, the players, the posters and standees are all relics now, much like me. Middle age creeps on and I swear in my head I'm still about 18. It's an odd situation to find yourself in when you suddenly realize that the zeitgeist you were part of is now a chapter in the history books. Or at least a page on Wikipedia if nothing else.

Amazingly, the last VCR wasn't the weirdest VHS news that year. A man from North Carolina, James Meyers, was pulled over by police for a broken brake light. It turned out they also had a warrant for his arrest due to… an overdue VHS tape he'd rented in 2002. The tape was, of all things, *Freddy Got Fingered.* The absurd situation resulted in Mr Meyers being taken to the station to be questioned and patted down! A court date was set up. The fact that the video store was long gone and the tape was missing yet all of this happened is absurd. Much like the end of the report, in which it was noted that *'Freddy…'* star Tom Green (yeah, I'd forgotten he existed too - I'm getting old) had called the guy in the middle of the night, recited a scene from the movie and offered to help with legal costs. Truth is often stranger than fiction.

An old VHS urban myth reared its stupid head again in 2016 when 'Black Diamond' Disney VHS tapes were said to be worth a fortune. They aren't. Cue loads of eBay listings asking thousands of dollars for them. The thing is, nobody actually bought them at that price. If you looked at the sold listings, they were generally selling in the US for about $25.

Stories like these continue to pop up to this day, with outrageous headlines claiming that THOSE VHS TAPES IN YOUR LOFT ARE WORTH MORE THAN YOUR HOUSE or some similar shit. They more than likely aren't. I hate to paraphrase internet trolls, but do your research.

One thing that was big for me personally in 2016 was the birth of the *VHS Ate My Brain* column in *Scream* horror magazine here in the UK. I was approached about doing something with them and decided to resurrect the first book as a column in the magazine. I wrote the first year of columns and then due to some personal stuff going on decided to bring it to an end and left the magazine. However, they continued the column without me, still entitled *VHS Ate My Brain*, with other people. It's still running right now. I'm not particularly thrilled that they still use the title as it's such a massive part of my life, but I want to be professional about it all. Thankfully the editions I have seen that were not written by me still carry the spirit I intended them to have so that's something.

2017 was a busy year for VHS awareness. In January, an art installation opened in Los Angeles that contained 14,000 copies of *Jerry Maguire* on VHS. I guess Hell does exist after all. Over in Northern Colorado however, media archivist Eddy Coloton was digitising artistic works that were shot on videotape, as were the independent 'XFR Collective', albeit a wider variety of tapes.

The Houston Chronicle published a quality article in which they interviewed Jason Champion of Champion Video, in which they managed to capture the real feeling of nostalgia and community that the VHS scene generates, as well as covering how the scene had grown. Reading it was a breath of fresh air for me, and a timely reminder that we weren't alone in our escapades, especially when mentioning how the *Horror VHS Collectors Unite!* Facebook page was - at that point - over 12,000 members strong. That group inspired my own VHS book, so hey, I guess something good has come out of Facebook after all.

There was a lot of talk about VHS tapes being digitised, several pieces on collectors and their video store recreations, and a few pieces on the more notorious of the VHS Facebook groups, such as the infamous *VHS Misfits* and dozens of others.

My friend Josh Schafer posted a great piece on his iconic Lunchmeat VHS site on the thrill of the hunt in 2017, which made me hanker for a good long hunt before I remembered I was in the UK which often feels like a lifeless misery lump on the world's ass and tapes are few and far between anywhere but the internet here.

The film *Videoman* (which I mentioned at the start of the book) arrived in 2018 and the director, Kristian, was interviewed by PopMatters. He discussed the themes of the film and the power of nostalgia, along with the bittersweet pangs of sadness that come with it.

I sort of get that, but I don't think it's something that affects every nostalgia junkie. For me, it's about appreciating these things I grew up with, but also finding things I never knew existed that came out in the same era. There's always something to discover. Just tonight for example I found an eighties movie I don't believe I've heard of before and have certainly never seen, namely the punk-themed drama *Smithereens* from 1983. Nostalgia offers so much more than just revisiting the same things over and over - you can greatly enrich your appreciation for an era by seeking out things that are new to you but have that same hit of vintage fun.

Later in 2018 the website Quartz ran an informative and pretty comprehensive look back at the video era, simply entitled 'VHS Tapes'. At the time of writing, it's still up and well worth a read.

In February 2019 the hipsters got in on the act when Urban Outfitters in the US started selling vintage VHS tapes for $40 a throw. More as kitsch trinkets than something that you'd find on a collector's shelf. This didn't sit well with me as it felt so fake.

On a more interesting note, early 2019 saw *Recorder: The Marion Stokes Story,* the documentary on the lady who recorded TV 24/7, was released to much acclaim.

A famous VHS-related story was reported in February 2019 surrounding a letter an eBay seller had received after selling a VCR to an older gent. The dude had written to the seller to thank him for selling the VCR as it had allowed him to view tapes from decades previous, including tapes featuring friends and family who had passed away. There's the magic of VHS for you right there - never mind news stories being captured. You could capture events exactly as they happened. Think of how beautiful it would be to see people who had passed away, captured happy at parties, weddings and more.

September 2019 saw an art exhibition in Wolverhampton themed around the lives of migrants display a VHS rental store element. Other news stories in 2019 included the sale of a massive library of boxing-themed VHS, documentaries and indie films still being released on VHS and the usual rash of 'these VHS tapes are worth money' type posts doing the rounds again, just as they do every couple of years.

Then came 2020 and the world changed. I won't go into what happened in much detail, but when Covid-19 spread across the globe and we locked ourselves indoors, life became a different game for a long while. To be perfectly honest, everything since then has been much of a blur. Some cool VHS things landed online that year, such as the piece on the Flickering Myth website on the joy of Orion Pictures, the low-budget *Rent-a-Pal* movie inspired by VHS, and various nostalgic web articles on the VHS era.

It felt like the first rumblings of longing for what became known as The Before Times, before masks and tests and jabs and social distancing. VHS tapes seemed like a relic of a safer, saner era. I totally understood that. I rediscovered several things from my younger years during the pandemic, including *Magic the Gathering, Warhammer 40,000*, comics, vintage sci-fi and countless other things that took my fancy during those strange non-days we lived through. I was put on the furlough payment scheme before ultimately losing the job I was working, but because we weren't travelling anywhere and had finally worked out how to budget properly, we were financially OK. It took its mental toll on us though, so the need for distraction was huge. I played countless hours of *Magic The Gathering: Arena* online, often late through the night. I painted *Warhammer* minis and went over rulebooks and websites and magazines and novels obsessively. I even made a Magic The Gathering YouTube show for a little while.

But while those interests were ultimately pretty fleeting, there were still those last few tapes I hadn't misguidedly sold off. There they were, waiting for me, ready to be played and enjoyed all over again. I opened a few cases and it dawned on me that I hadn't rewound some (yes yes, I know I'm evil) since before the pandemic had begun. I remember looking at them and thinking of the me that had been watching them before, the me that hadn't lost a job, the me that didn't have to socially distance, the me that had plans for the future and now those plans were even more vague.

I rewound the tapes and rediscovered them. Immediately I felt the remorse of having sold most of my most treasured tapes. It may seem silly to an outsider but I'm sure many tapeheads will relate. There's something you have a hankering to watch, but then you remember you sealed it up and shipped it out ages ago.

The world hadn't stopped, but it had changed. We had to live at a different pace. For some of us, that meant getting lost in the realms of nostalgia to a much greater extent. We couldn't go far, so the selling and trading groups came into their own, as did eBay and Amazon. We found a way to get our fix.

The world continued to find some content through VHS during the continued horrors of the pandemic. A *'Home Video Horrors'* calendar kicked off the year in style with a homage to classic VHS artwork. the *New York Times* posted yet another in the media's seemingly inexhaustible 'VHS tapes are worth money' dumpster fire of articles. As with many of these types of articles, it was best taken with a pinch of salt as to what tapes are actually worth money, as the market fluctuates at such a crazy pace it's hard to pin down.

Echoing earlier stories, a woman from Texas, Karen McBride, was horrified to find there was a warrant out for her arrest due to a *Sabrina the Teenage Witch* VHS tape she hadn't returned to the store since renting it 1999.

The video rental store had long since closed down, but hey, when would something like that make a difference? Crazy.

Speaking of crazy, 2022 certainly was. Two things stick out as being particularly dodgy for the VHS scene. Both incidents involved classic VHS tapes selling for a fortune, which caused a load of tapes to flood the market and once again give a skewed perception of VHS collecting and the value of tapes.

The two movies in question were *The Terminator* and *Back to the Future*, two evergreen titles that the public at large is totally aware of. A copy of *The Terminator* sold for $32,500, yes, but that tape was a first print in astonishingly good condition. A copy of *Back to the Future* sold for an eye-watering $75,000, but again this wasn't an average copy found in a closet - it was a graded and sealed copy signed by Biff Tannen actor Tom Wilson - and had come from his personal collection. As such, the tape had a direct link to the movie itself, hence the crazy price.

The problem was, most people who flung their tapes at eBay hadn't actually read the multiple articles about those sales and weren't aware of the special nature of them.

As such, the market saw an influx of tapes that sold for a few quid rather than a fortune.

Always take claims of tapes being worth a massive amount with a pinch of salt - there is always more to it. Those stories claiming that VHS tapes that many would have in their garage or in a cupboard are worth a fortune continued throughout 2023 as well, with outlets like the New York Post, Click Orlando, MoreFM and various other places yet again floating the notion that people were sitting on tapes worth thousands. These pieces were uniformly clickbait and little else.

Thankfully 2023 also brought some more interesting VHS content, such as the story of the dude in Florida who owns over 1,500 copies of *Titanic* on VHS, and would like to one day own one million copies of it. You do you, man!

Canadian comedy actor Pete Davidson floated that he had bought up thousands of sealed VHS tapes as an investment while being interviewed on *The Tonight Show with Jimmy Fallon*, much to the amusement of the audience and, no doubt, the annoyance of a lot of collectors.

SFGate published a lovely piece on the Basement VHS Club in San Francisco. The article, *'Really weird tapes: How these friends turned an SF basement into a VHS museum'* nicely shows off the grassroots DIY vibe of pretty much all of the

VHS scene as a whole, just making stuff happen because you think it would be cool.

The Washington Post published a great piece entitled *With VHS and video stores, 'Tapeheads' are fuelling an analogue revival*. This well-researched article included interview content with people like the wonderful Be Kind Video, Josh Schafer of Lunchmeat (there's an interview with Josh later on in this very volume as well), Whammy Analogue Media and more. The piece delves into the rise in retro media and why fans are developing more of an interest in tapes and the culture surrounding them. It shows the organic growth of the scene brought about by feeling jaded by streaming services and the disposable nature of so much media in the modern age.

There was one 2023 piece that really grabbed me and made me feel more than a little jealous. In July, horror site Bloody Disgusting posted a write-up of the yearly *VHS Fest*, this one having taken place at the Mahoning Drive-In Theatre in Pennsylvania. It talked about the brilliant three-day event, full of screenings and dealers and awesome people hanging out, including a few friends I saw in the accompanying photos. I am not aware of any UK-based VHS-centric events like this, and I am not sure if that's a failure on my part for not looking in the right places or if they just don't happen here. Maybe that's something I should be a part of if one happened here. Mind you, with zero event experience or indeed any useful experience that would help stage a movie gathering, I'd be lost. I supposed it'd be different if there was a community of like-minded individuals somewhere... oh wait.

Food for thought.

2024 thus far seems to be a year where the VHS community really gels. There are numerous channels, zines, groups, sites and more that are keeping the VHS dream alive in 2024 and I am so grateful for that. I may never find everyone who is keeping that flame burning, but the knowledge that there are other weirdos like us (yeah, I'm including you in that - look what you're reading!) is so reassuring. Tapes won't just be thrown in landfill. Films that never made it to disc won't completely vanish.

Something that has been of interest to me in the intervening years between my first exploration of the VHS scene and this one is that this niche interest hasn't really been lampooned or made fun of. There is a collective nostalgia for video tapes and video stores and as such it seems to have bypassed being mocked too much. That shared goodwill towards it seems to have spilt over to younger generations who, while they don't have the video store muscle memory, sort of get why these things matter.

While all of this was going on around the world, VHS collecting fandom continued to grow. Events around the world saw fans come together to hang out, trade and buy tapes. Groups on Facebook continued to thrive and expand, often focusing on an area of the world or a genre, pulling like-minded fans in. Tapes galore found their way onto eBay and Amazon and Facebook marketplace and everywhere else that people could buy and sell. CRT TVs started going up in price as demand rose for classic TVs for the real VHS experience - or indeed for playing retro video games in their native habitat. The hunger for tapes grew with the interest, with words like 'retro', 'eighties' and 'vintage' making people look at listings.

VHS continues to be talked about online, with pieces covering most watched tapes, the importance of the video rental stores, software plugins that give that authentic VHS look to things, even an account of grumpy director Martin Scorcese's voracious appetite for archiving TV broadcasts on VHS. Heck, I just this minute saw a piece talking about a new indie movie showing up on VHS, namely *The People's Joker.*

It really does feel that, while largely gone and very obsolete, VHS really hasn't been forgotten. Not only that, but it's often looked upon with fondness far outside of the collector scene.

A major element that has risen over the past few years, I'd say mainly since lockdown, has been the explosion of YouTube channels and podcasts covering VHS, retro movies and retro pop culture in general. Go put 'VHS' or 'retro horror movies' into YouTube, Spotify or whatever platforms you use and the results will no doubt bring up a wealth of things to dive into. I'll talk more about YouTube in a while.

The VHS scene didn't spill over fully into the popular zeitgeist (yet), but it never faltered and never went away. VHS collecting is like underground punk music. It's never cool enough for the mainstream but it never seems to fade away. It just carries on in its own crazy world, dancing to the tune of VCRs the world over. I love that.

Interlude
Fanboying at Rothrock and Zagarino

Please post any relevant questions in the chat and I will get to them if I can

Gareth Packham over on the Video Tasties channel is both a scholar and a gentleman. He has some incredible guests stop by his channel to talk about tapes, and has on several occasions let the standard slip by letting me come along and bring the tone down. On two streams he has had me come on to chat with guests I never thought I'd get to talk to in a million years. The first one was Cynthia Rothrock, the martial arts legend I obsessed over in the 90s thanks to films like *Lady Dragon, China O'Brien, Guardian Angel, Tiger Claws* and many more. She was doing guest spots on all manner of shows and channels and podcasts in support of the Kickstarter campaign for her film *Black Creek*, a martial arts action Western flick.

A message popped up from Gareth that it was time for me to show up, so on I went and immediately had to fight back the urge to gush fanboyisms at Cynthia. However, I did give in to some level of slightly awkward nerding out by informing her that as a teenager I had written a movie script I wanted her to be in. I had called it *KT, Biowarrior.* Get it? Like 'Katie'?

It was a story that would have been impossible to make, as it was pretty much just a series of fight scenes after an intro that explained KT was a cyborg. I don't think Cynthia was particularly impressed, so I moved on to my actual question.

I asked what the experience was like of taking on so many roles with *Black Creek,* from being its star, working on its script, producing, having a hand in the casting work and more. She immediately brightened and gave a heartfelt and interesting answer, explaining that she was applying all that she had learned over the years from working with others.

It was still proving to be a challenge but it was one she was relishing. That's very Cynthia. This is the lady who has amassed an incredible number of martial arts achievements throughout her career and worked with filmmakers all over the world on projects that have thrilled people for decades. It was a really special moment to me, one of those bucket list items you never think you'll live out.

Not long after this, Gareth got in touch again to tell me he was going to have Frank Zagarino on the show, and he wondered if I'd like to co-host that session. I jumped at the chance. Here was the inhuman cyborg killing machine from the *Project Shadowchaser* movies, all of which I'd rented in the VHS days. Of course, he has a filmography far longer than just those films, but those were the ones that I'd snapped up as a teenager.

Once it came around, the interview proved to be one of my favourite things I've done on YouTube. Frank was eloquent, open, warm and full of anecdotes about his career. He dealt with my incessant fanboying really well and was a pleasure to talk to. Not bad going for a killer cyborg. Mind you, the shock of bleached blonde hair he had in those films had been replaced by a far more sedate style here in the future. Oh well. He was still awesome.

Getting to talk to people who I idolised in my own little video world is a beautiful experience. Getting the chance to tell them they sparked my imagination and gave me some solace through a chaotic time of life. I couldn't be more grateful for these experiences, even if I make people cringe. I love this stuff and I'm proud of that. I'll never be ashamed of the things I love.

Chapter Nine
Brilliant additions to VHS/retro culture

As well as the things going on in the news that pertained to VHS collecting and associated culture, a great many VHS-related delights arrived that reminded people what a major aspect of our lives tapes once were. I'll give honourable mentions to *Adjust Your Tracking* and *Video Nasties: The Definitive Guide*, as I talked about those a lot in the first book. Those two pieces remain my favourites by far and I implore you to watch them both if you're yet to see them.

Adjust Your Tracking is a brilliant slice of DIY filmmaking made by VHS addicts, touring America to seek out the country's weirdest and greatest tapeheads. It's a weird watch for me as I knew a lot of the people that are interviewed in it in the early days of the Horror VHS Collectors Unite! Facebook page. I have rewatched it a few times over the last few months and even that ode to nostalgia is starting to develop a sheen of nostalgia of its own. Life is weird, man.

Plus if you look closely at the closing credits you'll see my name, so I'm biased towards loving it *(As an aside, I contributed to the Kickstarter for it, as I did with my only other movie credit appearance so far in a film I didn't make, namely Troma's Return To Nuke 'Em High Part 2. That flick had cameos from Stan Lee and Lemmy, so I like to think that, even in a tiny way, I got to be in something with Stan and Lemmy).*

Video Nasties: The Definitive Guide was an incredible 2010 box set containing 13 and a half hours of content including the documentary *Video Nasties: Moral Panic, Censorship and Videotape,* which remains the best look at the video nasties phenomenon made thus far. It was accompanied by every trailer from all 70+ films caught up in the video nasties controversy. It was followed in 2014 by a second part, entitled *Video Nasties: Draconian Days.* Again it was presented with a ton of extra material, and while not the masterpiece that the first one was, it was still an incredible piece of documentary filmmaking.

What I want to do here is talk about things that came out in the intervening decade between then and now that evoke that VHS scene excitement. They are presented here in no particular order. Something to note is that many documentaries and books will often cover the same ground but from a different perspective or with a different focus, and by checking out a variety of them you can get a real feel for what was going on. My focus is naturally mainly on horror and cult films, but there is always room to appreciate more mainstream content.

I'm a huge horror fan but I'm no snob when it comes to other genres. Actually, thinking about it, I probably am, but that's probably true for a lot of people. And anyway, horror movies are best, aren't they? Especially really bad ones. Those are definitely the best things of all. Whatever your particular preferred flavour of VHS culture, the things that follow are well worth your time.

VHS Nasty (2019)
This documentary got a lot right and presented the story of the VHS boom and its subsequent effect on popular culture very well. The people behind it clearly did a ton of research

and presented it here in a compelling fashion. One of the best VHS documentaries I've seen so far.

The Last Blockbuster (2020)

The aforementioned 2020 documentary is affectionate, entertaining and moving. It's the story of a video store, a family and the changing ways that entertainment is consumed. The film brings home what an important part of many lives the video store was, and not least the people who work in it. There's something optimistic and defiant in the family's steadfast refusal to let the store die, as it still has a place in the community.

At the time of writing this, the store is still alive. Their website offers Blockbuster T-shirts, hats and other merchandise, although the best one has to be a proper replica of a Blockbuster staff polo shirt.

That aside, it's a great documentary and any tapehead is sure to want to visit the place after watching it. Spend some time at the video store and discover it for yourself.

It Came From the Video Aisle (2017)

This book delves into the creation of Full Moon Features and goes seriously in-depth on the production of absolutely tons of their films. It's a truly hefty volume, co-written by a host of Full Moon and Charles Band aficionados, none of which pull any punches when they bring up the studio's lesser titles or the struggles that surrounded the production of many of their films.

In fact, the depth of detail that this book goes into really shows the love that was poured into the making of this crazy body of work that covers several genres and filled so

96

many video store racks. These films weren't just rush jobs to make a quick buck. They were made by talented people who needed to think on their feet and deliver decent products without the resources available to larger studios, and that ingenuity is addictive throughout.

A brilliant look into the career of Charles Band and his crazy studio.

Recorder: The Marion Stokes Project (2019)
This fascinating and emotional documentary tells the story of Marion Stokes, who recorded 840,000 hours of news coverage over a period of around 37 years.

She believed that a full archive of the news was the only way to preserve the truth in the face of so many different media viewpoints. A timely piece of filmmaking that addresses both her quest to save the truth and also the way in which we perceive media.

Analog Nightmares: The Shot on Video Horror Films of 1982-1995 (2018)
Edited by Richard Mogg
Okay, we're into serious territory now. This monstrous large format book clocks in at almost 500 pages and is the most comprehensive examination of SOV horror movies you'll ever find. Over 260 films are reviewed in detail and there are copious amounts of interviews and tons of photos too.

You won't find a more dedicated and insightful release on SOV horror anywhere. An incredible piece of work that acts as an indispensable guide to the lost art of SOV horror and as a masterpiece of cult film critique and appreciation. This book has become something of a shopping list, pointing me at dozens and dozens of titles I had never previously heard of. I know the tapes themselves would be almost impossible to get hold of, especially here in the UK, but I have found several films reviewed in the book on the Internet Archive as well as Youtube, Dailymotion and services like Plex and the Filmrise horror app.

Aesthetic Deviations (2023)
By Vincent A. Albarano
Despite the tiny print, this book is a masterclass example of how low-budget, often low-brow entertainment can be evaluated in a scholarly manner. It has the feel, attitude and style of a thesis, albeit a thesis peppered with stills and artwork from some of the craziest shot-on-video horror movies ever made.

But this goes deeper than just talking about the films themselves. This book goes deep into evaluating shot on video movies as an art form, as many capture elements of real life in their settings and their location footage, making them, weirdly, more realistic than bigger budget pictures.

The writing style may be a little dense for some tastes, but persevering with it reaps great rewards. A remarkably well-written and researched book on a remarkably weird niche corner of cinema. Fantastic.

Satanic Panic: Pop-Cultural Paranoia in the 1980s
Edited by Kier-La Janisse & Paul Corupe (2015)
That most eighties of cultural low points, the so-called Satanic Panic was hysteria generated by overbearing parents groups, evangelists and the media. It demonised

heavy metal, horror movies, Dungeons & Dragons and everything else that kids were enjoying at the time.

This great book takes you through the whole controversy, from the films and music, back-masked messages, sensationalist talk shows to the elements of the media that were built to perpetuate the panic, namely the Tom Hanks-featuring TV movie *Mazes & Monsters*, a cynical and laughably bad film about the dangers of fantasy role-playing games.

Over 360 pages or so, the book covers all of the ridiculous things that created the panic, including the real-life crimes that were then blamed on heavy metal, horror movies or D&D. At some points harrowing and other points hilarious, the book is consistently entertaining and eye-opening. The lies that were picked up and run with by mass media created a fallacy that damaged culture and damaged lives.

The Satanic Panic was a giant lie, and this fantastic book contains everything you need to know about the whole mess. It covers so many things I love, including a great section on *Trick or Treat (1986)*, so of course it gets a thumbs-up from me. Well-written and thoroughly researched, it's a damn fine thing.

VHS Lives: A Schlockumentary (2017)

Part of a slew of retro-themed documentaries that arrived since the impact that things like the seminal *Adjust Your Tracking* (2013), *VHS Lives* may be far too long at over two hours, but it makes those two hours pass well with a lot of detail and some impassioned research.

Covering the highs and lows of the VHS era, it features some fantastic cult video luminaries, such as David

DeCoteau, Jörg Buttgereit and SOV horror maker Scarlet Fry along with fanatics, writers and others in the know. The film is a solid watch but due to its run time does feel like it goes in circles a little. That said, it is definitely worth the time of the avid Tapehead.

Best. Movie. Year. Ever. (2019)
By Brian Raftery
What makes a movie good or bad is largely subjective (unless it's *Wishmaster 3: Devil Stone* - I really seem to have it in for that flick, don't I?). One viewer's masterpiece will be another viewer's unwatchable nonsense. 1999 was a weird year in film, but this book argues (quite well, it has to be said) that it was a landmark.

At one end of the spectrum, there were milestone films like *The Matrix, The Blair Witch Project, Office Space, The Sixth Sense* and *Being John Malkovich*. At the other end of the spectrum? *Star Wars Episode I: The Phantom Menace.* Yeah, it was a year of extremes.

It was also genuinely a pinnacle year in terms of cultural phenomena, and many would argue it was a pinnacle that the years since are yet to even come close to.

Raftery's book is a great blast of nostalgia that will cover the contents of many a VHS collector's library.

Are You Home Alone? (2016)
Edited by Amanda Reyes
TV movies were a strange beast, and this excellent book edited by Amanda Reyes covers the phenomenon of the American TV movie between 1964-1999 in fascinating detail. We didn't see all of these films on TV over here, but

100

several were packaged up as movies for the rental market, so we did get to glimpse some of this odd sorts of film to a limited extent. Obvious examples that made it to the UK would be the *IT* miniseries, the *Incredible Hulk* TV movies or even *Salem's Lot.*

This book takes us through decades of often-hastily-made TV movie treasures and turkeys. Many were intended as backdoor TV pilots rather than standalone films, offering a weird look at how different the pop culture landscape would have been if any of them had gone to series.

The films cover horror, thriller, romance, comedy, action, sci-fi and even the dreaded 'drama', and while I'm sure some of them were watchable, I bet this book is way more entertaining.

One Night Rental (2024)
Directed by Chris Annable
Not a documentary or a book or a podcast, but an actual movie shot in a video store - namely the 80s Video Shop that I keep banging on about. It's directed by Chris Annable from the shop itself and stars among its cast my buddy Rob Lane. It tells the story of, yup, Rob and Chris, two guys who run a video store. The film version of Chris is played by Bobby Furniss, who does a great job of capturing Chris's character.

I would liken the film to a working-class English version of Kevin Smith's glorious *Clerks*, mixed with a buddy action movie. Our fictional versions of Rob and Chris fall foul of a local bad guy and must fight to stay alive, along the way dealing with the parade of oddballs that head into the video shop. Waitasec, are they saying VHS fans are weird?

Well. Well, I never. I will have to have words.

Anyway.

The film works well both as an action-tinged buddy comedy and also as a giant, obvious love letter to video stores and loving cult films. There are absolutely shedloads of film references, and the setting of the shop adds authenticity to the low-budget madness. I love this film, and not just because I know the place and the guys who made it, but because it's a lot of fun and has been made with enormous amounts of passion and talent.

In some ways, *One Night Rental* is the perfect nod to the VHS scene, in that it was made by enthusiasts, much like so many other things that keep it alive. Those kids who grew up watching too many films on rough VHS tapes are now heading up the revival and appreciation of the medium. Fantastic.

VHS Ate My Brain: Revised Edition (2023)
By me
How could I not include this? I know I know, it's very self-serving, but the original *VHS Ate My Brain* was (probably) the first book ever released on the VHS scene, sold for a decade, spawned a magazine column and a podcast and kept me well-furnished with messages from readers around the world. It was a nexus for me, giving me a sense of belonging in a scene that was spread out far and wide. It changed my life.

I had always wanted to deal with the rough edges the original had, so I created a new edition with 80-something extra pages and a fully revised text. I wanted to offer a definitive version that would last another ten years. I hope I managed it.

YouTube channels covering VHS

Not strictly one thing in itself, I know. I'm talking about VHS-themed YouTube channels here as due to the nature of YouTube, channels are never set in stone and may well change within a couple of months of me putting this out. Channels end, channels change focus, and fans move on. That's how it is.

That said, there are some incredibly talented - not to mention prolific - VHS-themed content creators out there. The first that comes to mind, which may well be an obvious choice to many of you as well, would be Video Tasties. The channel is run by Gareth Packham, who is interviewed elsewhere in this book. As well as edited videos galore, he posts examinations of his extensive collection, reviews, live streams with other creators, interview live streams with VHS-era film stars and crew, watch party discussions and more. He's personable and relentless in his outpouring of quality content. Check him out.

Next up there's Fanzcene, who is a staunch supporter of physical media, constantly posting videos in support of physical formats and also co-hosting the *Physical Media show*. A passionate individual with some powerful arguments for the continued use of physical films rather than losing yourself in the mire of streaming services.

VHS Mikey is a big name to be aware of. Mikey has a huge personality and a very obvious love for the movies he talks about. Plus his YouTube set is the coolest out of all of us that do it. Mikey's videos are always fun, and that anarchic streak he has keeps everything moving along at an entertaining pace. The Troma of VHS YouTubers, and I mean that in the nicest way.

Masters of the 80s and Rob's Vintage Video also come to mind in terms of quality VHS-themed content, but there are so many more that it's pretty hard to find one that isn't entertaining.

What I find inspiring about the channels I follow is the passion for the medium and the sheer mass of knowledge that the people involved have. There are people on these channels who are way beyond my knowledge, and their excitement and drive to share that passion is infectious.

There are countless other VHS-era books, documentaries and channels out there to discover and get lost in. Others I would recommend include *VHS Forever: Psychotronic People, Barbarians at the Gates of Hollywood, Satan in the Celluloid, Wild & Crazy Guys, Chasing the 80s, Electric Boogaloo: The Wild Untold Story of Cannon Films, Bleeding Skull* (another great book on SOV horror) and many more. Take a look around at what the fans are saying about the titles here and find your own way through the crazy retro world we are living in.

Above all, have fun rediscovering, or indeed discovering anew.

Chapter Ten
The Stranger Things Effect

It's impossible to think about the rise of retro culture in recent years without acknowledging the cultural phenomenon of *Stranger Things,* the Netflix series devised by Matt and Ross Duffer, otherwise known as The Duffer Brothers. Debuting in 2016, throughout its existence it has turned talent like Millie Bobby Brown, Finn Wolfhard, Sadie Sink and Gaten Matarazzo into global stars and brought many classic 80s songs back into the wider consciousness.

Stranger Things has been such a massive success that it has not only inspired several imitators and retro aesthetics to become very popular, but it has forever changed the landscape of genre TV.

The fifth and final series is currently in production at the time of writing, and fans the world over are awaiting every update with excitement.

What is it about this show, which has been arguably rather patchy apart from, in my opinion, series 1 and series 4, that has so grabbed the zeitgeist?

Series 1 of *Stranger Things* introduced us to the central characters, a bunch of likeable nerdy kids, and the psychically powered Eleven, along with the alternate world known as The Upside Down and the strange goings on in the laboratories where Eleven and others like her were held prisoner.

That first series felt to me like it was steeped in the work of Stephen King (somewhat akin to a sci-fi-tinged *Stand By Me*). It established the fictional town of Hawkins very well, and those central characters were so well-played and well-developed that viewers were on board straight away. As with many works by Stephen King, the gradual and subtle changes from a mundane story of everyday life into one touched by the supernatural were handled beautifully.

Stranger Things kicked off a wave of 80s nostalgia that had been bubbling up for a while but had never really ignited. Then came this show and everything blew up. The fashions, music and pop culture references were spot on, and as the series developed it brought things like arcades, shopping mall photo sessions and dodgy haircuts very much to the fore of cultural awareness.

It also dispelled the notion that everything in the eighties was drenched in neon. Dude, everything in the home in the eighties was brown. Brown walls. Brown furniture. Brown carpets. Brown brown brown. Apart from bathrooms, which over here were often a fine shade of avocado and smelled of chemicals that were nowhere near the 'pine' scent stated on their bottles and cans.

By pitting a group of relatable kids against a dark force, Stranger Things evokes a ton of VHS-era classics like *Goonies, Explorers*, the aforementioned *Stand By Me, IT,* and even stuff like *The Monster Squad* or *The Gate.*

To me that's one of the reasons *Stranger Things* works so well - the makers understand the power of those old titles, the books, the comics, the tabletop games, the whole zeitgeist of the era, and were able to translate that to something a modern audience wouldn't just enjoy, but truly become obsessed with.

Its cross-generational appeal gave the old viewers a huge hit of nostalgia and young viewers a compelling glimpse at an era they hear so much about. Also, to me anyway, it's great to watch something without the merest hint of smartphones or social media. That alone is refreshing in these chaotic and relentless days.

Stranger Things also kicked off a wave of imitators. Some were good, some were bad, but all of them had clear influences from the Duffer Brothers' creation. Some took inspiration from media that far predated *Stranger Things*, but the influence on how they were made is clear.

Fear Street, a trilogy of movies inspired by RL Stine's classic young readers' novels, had a strong *Stranger Things* vibe, even casting Max from Stranger Things, Sadie Sink, in a leading role. Others that came in the wake of the show included things like *My Best Friend's Exorcism* (adapted from the novel by Grady Hendrix), *Paper Girls, Riverdale, Dark, Totally Killer*, the big screen remake duology of Stephen King's *IT*, the revivals of *Creepshow, Goosebumps* and many others.

One huge example of the *Stranger Things* effect is the nostalgia fest that is *Ghostbusters: Afterlife*. That long-awaited continuation of the original *Ghostbusters* canon was oozing with influences from Hawkins. The small town setting. The group of young main characters (including Finn Wolfhard from *Stranger Things* itself), the gradual mystery of the supernatural events unfolding around them and the formation of a team, it was right out of the *Stranger Things* playbook. You know what? I was fine with that. It had enough reverence for the original that I think it did the franchise proud. That has since been followed by *Ghostbusters: Frozen Empire*, which intentionally leans heavily into the style of the 1980s cartoon *The Real Ghostbusters*.

A hugely positive influence that the show has had has been a reimagining of how friendships are depicted onscreen. By emphasizing those bonds of friendship and loyalty against insane odds, episodes have become classic milestones in the modern pop cultural pantheon and influenced a new generation of stories.

It's actually weird to think that just a few years ago nobody had heard of *Stranger Things,* but it has been a franchise that has really caught the imagination of the masses and in its own way directed them to maybe check out some of the titles that inspired it. That's cool by me.

Chapter Eleven
Full Moon Overhead

Full Moon Features have a lot to answer for. I wrote about my love for them in the first book and have covered their stuff extensively on YouTube, but that won't stop me mentioning them here. You see, I really, really want to write a movie for Full Moon Features. They were the home of a great many favourites of mine and I have long since admired their audacity in getting the most out of what many would see as meagre budgets.

I have several ideas for Full Moon style movies on a budget, as well as ideas for sequels to many of their one-off properties. I mean, sequels have a built-in audience so are a win-win to me, even if some see them as a lesser product. I don't share that opinion. Sign me up. Sequels ahoy!

One problem that may get in my way is that I generally want to write sequels to things that weren't that beloved in the first place, such as *Arcade*, the 1993 teen sci-fi thriller that featured Megan Ward, Seth Green and John DeLancie among its cast. That film had a troubled production, depending on what you read. Its story of teens getting caught up in the virtual reality world of a sentient video game was ahead of its time in my opinion, but the visuals did leave something to be desired.

Parts of the film take place in the virtual reality world, which naturally has some similarities to *Tron*, which was released by some little company called Disney. The original version of the CGI effects were alleged to be too similar to *Tron*'s iconic suits, light cycles and scenery, thus meaning they had to be remade quickly.

Whatever the background to that story, the finished film was one that I took to straight away. It had all of the things that made a fantasy-tinged teen film exciting to me. The kids weren't being listened to for most of the movie, even when their friends start disappearing. The main character of Alex (Megan Ward) had genuine trauma in her life which continued to haunt her. The characters were largely likeable and came across as an actual group of friends instead of a bunch of stage kids thrown together and told to act.

Eventually - spoiler alert - the remaining friends have to enter the virtual reality world of Arcade's living mind in order to rescue their friends and save the day before the murderous machine can cause any more harm.

Despite my love for it, I totally acknowledge that it doesn't have a brilliant reputation amongst B-movie lovers, with many putting it down for the effects, the budget or the script. I totally respect those opinions, especially as I know they're full of shit.

A sequel, to me, is ripe to be made right now. Think of what Arcade could get up to if it was uploaded to the internet on some retro game site or something. Think of what the violent living consciousness could do if it had access to every home, every pocket device, every TV. The story could be limited to a few locations while a few people in the know try to stop its consciousness from being set free online. Say it found its way onto a college server, it could take people over to be its physical army while the good guys find a way to get rid of it.

How would I end the movie? I have an idea that links it to the first movie but won't mention it here as I may need it at some point, ha! Make your own stuff!

What drives me to want to write low-budget movies rather than big blockbusters or serious dramas? I have nothing against either, but it's those crazy little films like *Arcade* that get me excited. I mean, the first one was written by David S Goyer (the *Dark Knight trilogy*, *Blade*, etc), so it definitely has some merit. The film was directed by the late Albert Pyun, who I maintain never got the respect he deserved.

Known for films like *Cyborg, Nemesis, Radioactive Dreams, Vicious Lips, The Sword and the Sorcerer,* the 1990 *Captain America* movie and many more, Albert was a gifted filmmaker who I think got stuck with low budgets so many times that a wider audience struggled to take him seriously enough.

Just before he passed away, I was able to get a message to him. His wife, Cynthia, had opened a public Facebook post on which fans could send Albert messages that she would read to him.

I sent a message and I like to think it was read out to him. It may not have, but I wanted to send a few words.

It was an act that brought some stuff into sharper focus. It reminded me that the figures behind the cult cinema I grew up on are human, that they age, they get sick and unfortunately, in the case of Mr Pyun, they pass away. Times and circumstances change. It made me think of my own mortality. What am I leaving behind to let the world know I was here?

Maybe the books, maybe the magazines or comics I've done. I have been lucky enough to make a tiny mark on the things that are important to me, and that's a great feeling.

Over everything, my sons and my wife are my world. I create to calm my chaotic neurodivergent mind a bit, but I hope that one day if the kids read the things I did, they'll get a better understanding of the person I am and the person I was when they were growing up.

All of which is a very roundabout way of saying 'I still want to write a Full Moon movie. Or two. Or three.'

Maybe so, at the very least, I can create something that goes directly to freaks like me.

It's always been the same to me. Everything that brings me pleasure eventually ends up being something I want to be involved with. Music. Films. Comics. Magazines. I don't just want to consume the stuff. I want to be a part of it. I want to lose myself in it and make my mark. This desire has resulted in some crazy adventures over the years, from DJing in packed alternative clubs, playing onstage with bands, location shoots for zero-budget films, recording albums, writing for superheroes and much more. Everything came from wanting to join in. Wanting those on the inside to know my name.

So I'm writing a sequel to *Arcade*.

That is to say, not for Full Moon. I am in no way affiliated with them, as much as I would like to be, and am doing it solely for fun. It's not one I'll try to make or send to them. Well, not unless they asked to see it.

I came up with a plot that would connect the original film to the modern age and would be set in very limited locations with a small cast and some big ideas. I got to work, fleshing out the story into a synopsis before getting underway with a few pages at a time.

Why bother? I'm not going to make money from it or see it get made, so why spend the time writing it?

That boils down to me just wanting an *Arcade* sequel to exist, even just as a spec script in my Google Drive. I'm having fun with it.

I did end up making a trailer for it, though.

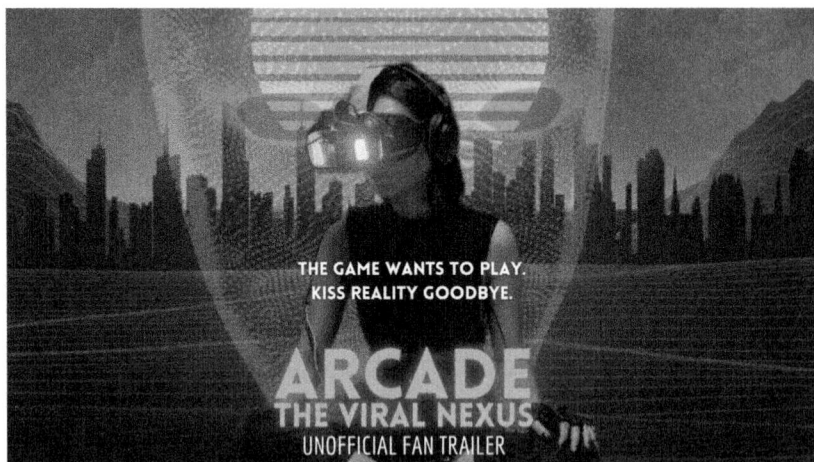

We were snowed in one Sunday, and plans for the day were scuppered by treacherous weather conditions. We decided to stay home. The kids played video games and watched streaming stuff. We read, cooked and hung out. I had a spark of inspiration regarding the *Arcade* sequel script and had to open the laptop and put something together, mainly with the hope of passing a few hours while we were stuck inside.

I sourced a bunch of stock footage, animations and music from free online outlets, then found an AI voice generator that would supply lines of dialogue as different characters. I cut it all together, including some stills from the original movie in the intro and sat back to watch a teaser for my very own sequel, now entitled *Arcade: The Viral Nexus*.

Once I'd shared it on Facebook in the Full Moon fan groups I'm in and on my own page, I added a disclaimer to the start of the video and posted it to YouTube. I know not many people will ever see it, but to me, it's a little taste of what could happen in a sequel and to me it feels like there's a bit more *Arcade* out there now.

Doing so made me think of all of those straight-to-video filmmakers I had grown up watching the work of, doing their best to make something worthwhile even though the audience wasn't likely to be huge.

The script continues to take shape. It's completely a piece of fan fiction, but heck, it's a ton of fun getting to step into a playground I'd admired for so long.

I would have no problem with it getting picked up, of course, but just by doing it, I feel like I'm contributing to the thing I love.

Interlude
VHS cake

My wife had a custom VHS tape birthday cake made for me. It's almost like she knows what I like or something! It was made by Amy's Cake Corner and it was the BEST. I posted these photos on social media and several people thought it was an actual tape as they scrolled past. In reality, it was a giant chocolate cake, which is probably the only way I could get excited about a tape that didn't have a film on it.

I mean, look at that. It's glorious. Thankfully it did not taste like magnetic tape, but it did taste like the tortured souls of my enemies, strapped to chairs and forced to watch the whole *Police Academy* franchise. On a loop. Imagine the torture every time you got around to *Mission to Moscow*.
   Terrifying.

Chapter Twelve
My new VHS mission

I've regretted selling off my original collection almost constantly since I did it. It didn't happen all at once, rather the collection shrank a bit when I sold off some tapes that weren't essential, then a few more, then some of the more treasured titles, and then suddenly I didn't have any tapes on display at all. A few stragglers remained in boxes in the loft, but I think I had reached a point where I needed a break from it all. I think maybe I'd taken it too far and had swamped the house with hundreds of tapes that I wasn't particularly attached to. I needed the money in many cases, with things like birthdays, Christmas, bills, the need for new clothes and whatnot getting in the way of my enjoyment like an angry grownup demanding I tidy my room.

Brown package after brown package was shipped out to collectors all over the country. Slowly the stash wasted away to almost nothing. It gave me a terrible twinge of seller's remorse every time I sealed up tapes that were like old friends in cardboard and bubble wrap and addressed them to others who would love them and not betray them as I had.

Naturally, after years without them, the desire to get at least some of them back into my collection is stronger than ever. I'll never have a massive collection again, but I would like a collection that speaks to me.

We had fitted wardrobes put into our master bedroom a few months ago, specifically designed so that, while the sides contain substantial wardrobe space for my wife and me, the central section that is usually hidden by a huge mirror can slide aside to reveal my Planet Hex YouTube set. The custom shelving units are filled with ex-rental tapes, some mass-market tapes, some tapes I recorded off the TV, bits of memorabilia, my 'On Air' neon sign and a selection of brand-adjacent DVDS.

Those shelves, one day, will just be filled with neat rows of ex-rental big box VHS tapes. That's the goal. They'll be uniform in size even though they won't be in alphabetical order. I don't do that. Things are usually arranged in order of my personal hierarchy rather than an actual filing system. The tapes I like the most will be grouped together, and in those groups there may be a rough theme, such as horror, Full Moon movies or a particular franchise, but for the most part, they are ordered by personal preference.

Will I buy back all the titles I sold off? No, I doubt it. Just some key titles that I particularly miss.

The problem is that a lot of those tapes have doubled or even tripled in price since the dark days of my selling spree. Tapes like *The Video Dead*, *Neon Maniacs*, *Return of the*

Living Dead (with the Graham Humphreys art cover) and a few others are high on my list, but their current prices really put me off. I can't justify a huge outlay for a video library, so I have to keep searching for grails at a low price. Thankfully that is starting to pay off, with some key tapes finally back in my collection after the late-night searches I've been recording for my YouTube channel. Recent acquisitions include *Necropolis, Shadowzone* and *Terror Vision*, albeit with a damaged cover on the latter.

I have accepted that an appreciation of the VHS era and its films is about more than just having the tapes. I still buy DVDs and Blu-rays of certain video-era titles as they are more accessible on a budget. They'll never hold the same magic as ex-rental tapes, but they allow me to have a copy of stuff I love, and that's a great feeling. At the time of writing, my two most recent Blu-rays have been *Ghoulies* and *Streets of Fire*, two very different titles that I wanted to enjoy again without the hefty price tag of tracking down ex-rentals. I doubt I'll ever stop loving tapes and other ephemera of the era, but these days I am less averse to disc-based copies. They're still better, to me anyway, than watching via streaming services.

I feel that my new VHS mission has moved beyond just owning tapes. Right now I'm into spreading the word about the format and choice of titles that it exposed me to. I'm determined not to let the video era die and be forgotten. Seeing that I'm not alone in that has been wonderful, with so many YouTube channels, books, podcasts, documentaries and everything else out there holding the line against the march of time. Nostalgia has its uses, and letting people know there was a format that was at the top of the industry

120

for absolutely ages helps to speak out against disposable content culture and the sanitisation of the media we can take in.

Chapter Thirteen
Delving into SOV horror

Through my years as a devout - and occasionally lapsed - tapehead, I have heard many legends of the insane SOV (shot on video) horror movies that had been quite a big part of the VHS boom over in America. We didn't get many of those films over here as, well, we're a bit shit at everything cool, to be honest. I have previously lamented the fact that it was nigh on impossible to see US-made SOV horror over here in the UK.

The more I would read about these crazy films in social media groups, on websites and in books such as the frankly incredible *Analog Nightmares: The shot on video horror films of 1982-1995*, the more I wanted to sample some for myself.

The hyperbole was running rife. Films like *Video Violence, 555, Cannibal Campout, Tales from the Quadead Zone* and the outstandingly dodgy *Black Devil Doll From Hell* would be spoken about as though they were lost masterpieces, or at least a delicious secret to be shared amongst just a few diehard tapeheads that didn't care if something was terrible as long as they could watch a movie. As I identified with that latter group, I quickly developed an ongoing interest in seeing some of these flicks. Even if it was just so I could say I'd seen them. It was slightly awkward though, as no matter how much interest I had in them, SOV horror movies were something for American collectors.

That's not to say that SOV movies weren't made elsewhere, but the majority of the films that there has been a lot of chat about are those made in the States. I would wager that video camera equipment was more readily available over there, hence the torrent of American independent titles that would find their way into independent video rental stores and into collections via the classified pages of magazines and fanzines.

While browsing the Internet Archive, I was delighted to discover that a great selection of SOV horror flicks from throughout the era, including many of the heavy hitters, were available to view for free on that most odd of sites. I went into something of a frenzy, downloading and watching dozens of these things. I had found the motherlode of an arm of 80s/90s genre cinema that I had previously never had access to. I have never used file-sharing sites or apps, so I had never been exposed to the delights of *Dead Girls, Soul of a Demon* or *Psycho Sisters* before. I remedied that and must say the experience has been thoroughly enjoyable.

According to *Aesthetic Deviations: A Critical View of American Shot on Video Horror 1984-1994* by Vincent A. Albarano, the wave of zero-budget movies that found space on video store shelves would often garner complaints from those who had rented them. Behind the garish covers, the expectation had been for something above the level of consumer camcorders, in-camera mics, monotonous Casio keyboard scores, a lack of any acting ability and a general DIY feeling. It was an example of how video stores levelled the playing field between glossy Hollywood movies and low/no-budget films. If customers rented a SOV horror movie without knowing the limitations of what they were going to watch, you can bet they would be confused and probably pretty angry to find they'd rented something shot in a backyard with some mates and a bucket of ketchup.

But the modern tapehead is a very different beast to a general consumer. We know what to expect from these things and when they're even worse than we expected them to be, we're delighted.

Notable titles of the SOV horror pantheon include early efforts like *Boardinghouse* and *Blood Cult*, the former of which was one of the earliest SOV horror movies ever made, while the latter was advertised as 'the first feature film made for the home video market'.

As SOV features of different genres started to find their way onto rental store shelves, they quickly gained a reputation for being amateurish films with very little of any real merit. They were filmed with cheap consumer equipment, starring people who couldn't act, reciting lines written by people who didn't know how to put a script together and boasted zero in the way of production values.

So, considering all of these issues that consumers raised with the cheap product they were paying to rent, how come SOV movies - and in particular horror - still find an audience even now?

There is an undeniable something about these films that - once you have a taste for them - it makes them utterly compelling. One aspect that I find fascinating is what's going on in the background of these films. They were more often than not made without permits to shoot a film anywhere so everything you see going on in the background in outdoor scenes is real life and real people. Cast members playing characters are surrounded by people, cars, families that are just going about their daily lives, unaware they are showing up in the background of a splatter epic or a thriller.

By doing this, these films, even the very worst of them, are historical documents that capture a period in time in its rawest, truest form. It was really the first era where this was possible for the public to do. Just think of the countless tapes out there somewhere. There are places where you could probably create a multi-camera VR experience just from the VHS shot in them alone.

Video Violence and *Video Violence 2,* both available to see on the Internet Archive, are excellent examples of the above in action, as they largely take place in a video store stuffed with enticing tapes and posters. Those films pre-empt the found footage genre nicely (yes, I know Ruggero Deodato got there first with *Cannibal Holocaust*), when the video store owners come across tapes of apparent torture and murder being carried out somewhere nearby. They are very much of their time, and as far as SOV movies go, both have something going for them in terms of cinematography, such as it is. Some thought has been put into those films even if money wasn't.

That people went out there and made these things with little or no money and still managed to get a finished product out to stores is impressive, especially when you consider the analogue methods they had to use for everything.

In the monster of a book I just mentioned that is the 486-page *Analog Nightmares: The shot on video horror films of 1982-1995* by Richard Mogg, over 260 SOV horror flicks are reviewed and many creators are interviewed. The fact that these tiny productions and their limited distribution is still cause for discussion here in the 2020s says something about the cultural impact they had. They were often far from great films, but they had something going for them, even if it was just great cover art.

Am I arguing that films like *Scarlet Fry's Horrorama, Splatter Farm, The Brainsucker, Trashcans of Terror* and their ilk are important milestones in cinematic history? I would argue that taken as a movement, these films are definitely an important milestone. Moviemaking was put into the hands of the fans for the first time ever, and the explosion in these productions across the world had to count for something.

People were getting to make things on their own terms, without the intrusion of studios or producers that would try to steer them in more commercial directions. SOV movies were a pure form of expression in that their creators just went for it, just with the intention of making something, be it good or bad. Some of the SOV scene regulars became incredibly prolific filmmakers, such as the Polonia brothers, who would become stalwarts of the scene with their many, many films.

Whether you see SOV films as the worst kind of junk or a gallery of unsung classics, it has to be argued that they have merit. They were finished. They got made. Film lovers and amateur performers got together and thrashed out a story and managed to pull it together into something resembling a film.

Be it *Sledgehammer, Black Devil Doll From Hell, Boardinghouse, The Burning Moon* or any of the other countless titles that arrived in the SOV boom, they managed to find an audience, albeit niche.

Here's a list of 25 SOV horror movies that I believe would give you a good overall feel for the subgenre.

Sledgehammer (1983)
Boardinghouse (1982)
Cannibal Campout (1988)
Woodchipper Massacre (1988)
Video Violence (1987)
Black Devil Doll from Hell (1984)
Killing Spree (1987)
Spine (1986)
The Basement (1989)
Video Violence 2 (1987)
Redneck Zombies (1987)
The Dead Next Door (1989)
Splatter Farm (1987)
The Burning Moon (1992)
Blood Cult (1985)
The Burning Moon (1997)
Shatter Dead (1994)
Feeders (1996)
Hellroller (1992)
Things (1989)
Crazy Fat Ethel II (1987)
Psycho Sisters (1998)
555 (1988)
Demon Queen (1987)
Tales From the Quadead Zone (1987)

If you come out of the other side of a SOV horror journey, you will come out as a changed person. I do apologise. I didn't say they were good, did I?

Oh, wait.

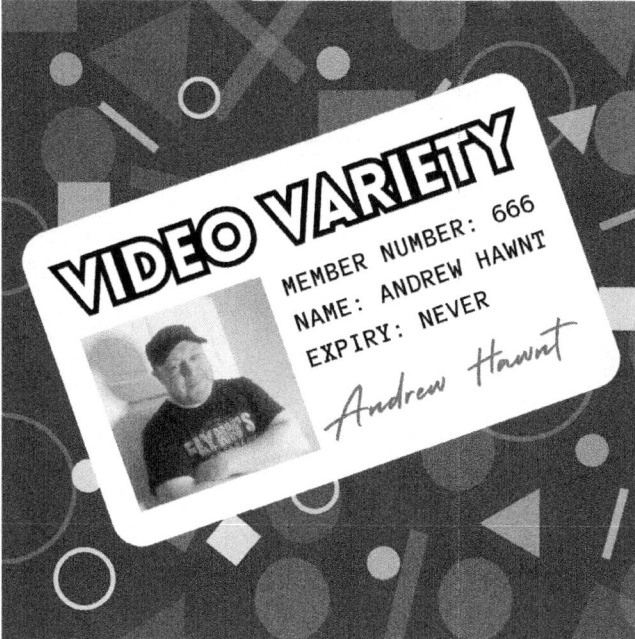

Chapter Fourteen
The growing importance of physical media

I am turning into an old man. I know. My mid-forties are here and with them has come a growing distrust of our march towards a wholly digital society. As a dad, I've been gullible enough to sign up for way too many streaming services to meet the very particular interests of the kids, my wife and occasionally myself. And yet, despite having almost a dozen paid services and twenty or thirty free services at my disposal, I increasingly find myself unable to choose something to enjoy. My watch lists are massive on each platform, and I swear I spend more time adding things to those lists than actually watching anything new. Often I can be found deep in the bowels of the free streaming services that are full of low-grade junk because that's what I cut my teeth on as a young film fan.

But it's not just the ludicrous - and often daunting - amount of choice available to us that doesn't sit well with me. I do enjoy having the services and what they offer and have spent many long evenings in their company, but it's not the content itself that unsettles me.

I do not enjoy being observed by an algorithm. I love watching films and TV shows and revisiting things that I'd seen while growing up, but I don't like knowing that everything I was is being observed and catalogued in order to make tailored advertising more tailored and more, erm, advertise-y. Knowing that my every move on these services will lead to similar - often lesser- product being wafted in my face isn't fun, especially when I remember the video shop years so clearly. The only people who knew what I'd watched then were the counter staff, and it was only recorded on my member card or their rudimentary computer.

Here and now I am but a droplet in a sea of digital noise, my viewing and listening habits being listed and circulated and connected to the adverts that will likely be the most enticing. I never felt like that when I was picking up tapes from Metro Video. Mind you, considering some of the shit I rented, it's probably for the best that nobody knew.

Another thing is that when I've watched something like a new horror movie or an old exploitation or cult film, the things that come up as suggestions for other stuff I may enjoy are usually wildly inappropriate for the kids to see. This leads to some awkward conversations. I really need to look through the settings and see what I can turn off.

Anyway. The other major factor in me holding onto the belief that physical media is king is the availability of what I want to see. Now that we are at the point where individual studios and distributors have their own streaming services, it's often impossible to see a particular title without forking out yet more money to subscribe to yet another service. Yes, there are free trials with many of these services, but it's easy to miss the cut-off point and wind up with more bills.

This practice of studios having their own services seems counterproductive to me. It could be argued that they would get more streams if their content was on a larger service, but I guess it all comes down to how much money can be squeezed out of the consumer before they run out of coin. If titles were all on larger services, then those platforms would take a chunk out of the studios' income in processing fees.

So ultimately, we pay a fortune to watch the things we like, the studios get more money from us and then what happens? The lifespan of a lot of the stuff we like is short. Titles get taken down. Things on digital platforms are prone to vanishing behind a paywall or just vanishing altogether. There's no ownership. You're just borrowing. Renting.

But Andrew, isn't that what you did at video stores in the increasingly distant past? Yes, it is, but we didn't have to go to an MGM video store, a Paramount video store, an Apple video store and so on. We would go to one place with one membership and everything was there for the taking.

To get me interested in a streaming service, it has to offer a hell of a lot for the price. The price also has to be right.

Thankfully, an old favourite production company has got the balance perfectly right, so I will use them as an example. Full Moon Features (yep, they do keep popping up here don't they?). The Full Moon Features app subscription is priced low, but for that fee, you get a hell of a lot of content. As well as the classic Full Moon movies library there are exclusive new films each month, shorts, interviews, bonus material and a library of related films the studio didn't make but appeal to their demographic.

There are indie productions, grindhouse favourites, world cinema and more, not to mention all of the content from Full Moon's spinoff labels. It offers the right amount of value for the cost that the company is asking for.

Aside from a few chewed tapes and scratched discs over the years, physical media has never let me down.

Has there been a change in how physical media is perceived in the last ten years? Absolutely. Ten years ago physical media was dying on its arse one way or another as the dawn of online video was in full swing. Streaming platforms felt like they were in their infancy and were exciting new things to enjoy for many people.

I won't deny that convenience is a great thing. Being able to fill my phone or a tablet with films for long journeys or commuting or just relaxing with (sporting headphones if the kids are yelling while on consoles) is a great thing and something I'm grateful for. That said, physical media should not be brushed aside as something from a previous era. Physical media won't let you down if your internet fails or the streaming service crashes. It won't snitch on you to your family when you've watched a gory slasher by suggesting other gory slashers. It also won't randomly vanish altogether like so many films and shows do at present.

Am I against streaming? No, it certainly has its place, as do all forms of media and all of the digital progress that has been made in such a short period of time. What I am against is the monetisation of our habits, our interests and our very being. Everything we do is ripe to be used in advertising, and it gets to a point where I have to take a digital detox now and again. I'm actually having one while I write this. I remove social media apps from my phone (apart from YouTube, because YouTube is a wonderful thing) and I exist without them for a week or so at a time. I may check in on the laptop once, but that's it. It gives me a break from the barrage of LOOK AT ME BUY THIS SUBSCRIBE HERE LOOK AT MY PATREON noise that otherwise fills my days.

I'd much rather put a video on.

During the VHS era, browsing the racks at your local video store for a ridiculous amount of time felt natural. I always loved the time I spent in those places, even if the racks were heaving with things I'd already seen or had little interest in. I could happily spend ages considering the mix of tapes I wanted to pick up for that night's binge. That browsing time felt like I was part of a scene, joining in with a massive hobby that was shared by millions. It was an essential part of the experience.

Dear reader, sitting scrolling through pages and pages of streaming service fodder does not hold the same pleasure. In fact, it can result in me getting pissed off with the whole thing and giving up, instead firing up a tape or a DVD or Blu-Ray. Why does it wind me up so much when I would happily spend hours standing in a shop, staring at the racks? Is it down to a collection of physical media being finite, limiting the number of choices that can be made? Is it because so much streaming content now is pretty interchangeable?

At the risk of sounding like Grandpa Simpson shouting at clouds, it felt different back in the day. There was excitement in going to a video shop that streaming services cannot replicate. It all feels like much of a muchness right now, with increasingly more streaming services offering ever-expanding catalogues of stuff that rarely warrants sitting through.

Something I have been enjoying of late is *The Physical Media Show* over on YouTube, which brings together a number of VHS and movie nerds for bumper-length videos chatting about the pros and cons of streaming media and why physical media is growing in importance once again. Episodes often run in excess of three hours and cover all manner of topics from the films across many genres and formats to the state of the industry, streaming media, production companies and more.

As with any YouTube channel, I don't always agree with what is being said, and that's fine. Nobody said we all had to like the same thing. However, what is overwhelmingly obvious with the opinions shared on the show and by the viewers of it clearly demonstrate there is an appetite for physical media even now.

I have the Arrow Video Blu-Ray box set that came out not so long ago which contains five movies from the Empire Pictures label, which was run by Charles Band prior to him starting Full Moon features and giving me something else to obsess over. That box set contains *The Dungeonmaster, Robot Jox, Arena, Cellar Dweller* and *Dolls*, all remastered and all sporting some incredible extras. I bring this up because it's a great example of a company that understands its audience and the market at present. The extras on the discs are excellent, and the alternate cuts of things like *The Dungeonmaster* (it includes both the *Ragewar* cut of the film and the alternate *Ragewar: The Trials of Excalibrate* cut as well as the main one). Including extras like these adds a lot of value to the fans out there. They may already own the films on DVD or - even better - VHS, so what would make us part with our cash? New restored versions of the films and a bunch of extras. It works. It sells these things to us.

I am under no illusion that physical media will ever be the dominant format for consuming media again, but if we reframe how we perceive that physical media and the market that it is aimed at, I believe we'll see even more of a boom in titles that are oozing with enticing extras. It's that reframing that will see physical media become more of a trusted option again. An alternative to the endless sea of expensive streaming services that clog our devices and drain our bank accounts.

A meme was doing the rounds on the internet recently that said 'How long until someone bundles the streaming services together and reinvents cable?' That really struck home. A package of services was far easier for family budgets to manage and delivered a great service.

I can't see the streaming era having the same nostalgia factor in years to come. Imagine looking back over the hours you spent flicking through stuff you didn't want to watch. Hours spent looking through stuff that is costing you money to not watch.

All of this tells me that, by giving us so much choice, the streaming services have actually taken away the ability for us to choose not to pay for content we don't consume.

Interlude
Talking Tapes for the Faithful Few

Thank you. Thank you for sticking by me while I make my videos and figure out how to get stuff out to you in the best way I can manage. I started my YouTube channel, like many people, in the dark days of 2020 as a form of lockdown escapism. I ran a *Magic The Gathering* show called *Turn One Shock* for 24 episodes before wanting to do something more varied and more personal. That's why *Planet Hex* became a thing.

But why make videos on VHS tapes? Because I want to be part of a scene that means so much to me and has done for many years. The things people are doing to maintain and develop this scene astound me on a daily basis and I'm proud to say I am an absolute addict.

I have a small but dedicated following on my Planet Hex YouTube channel. I really appreciate it that anyone watches my stuff at all. I talk about a lot of things on there that relate to pop culture, but it's always the VHS-themed videos that people seem to enjoy the most, hence me making so many

137

of them. I'm fine with that, as I love tapes. Just in case you hadn't figured that out by now.

Is it difficult coming up with ideas for tape talk week in, week out? No, it really isn't. There is so much to share about these old movies and this format that it never gets stale. I keep discovering things I haven't heard of before and keep rediscovering things that I want to share and talk about. The fact that anyone at all watches my endless online VHS hunt videos or the videos where I'm out hunting for films and other retro goodness in the wilds of Nottingham, Sheffield and elsewhere amazes me. I'm really grateful.

There's no glamour to what I do. The videos are all made with free assets, free music and free software. The ones that aren't filmed directly on my laptop are shot with two phones. I have a studio setup with a mic, lights, a backdrop and all that good stuff, but none of it is high-end. I'm not doing this stuff in order to show off an amazing filming setup or ultra-flashy visuals. I'm doing it to share my love for old films, weird collectables and nerd culture in general, with sprinklings of music talk, comics and the writing life.

I would imagine my audience are rather similar to me. they likely wear pop culture or music shirts, Vans (or Converse), caps and seem to have perpetual stubble. I doubt they all have the same caffeine addiction or baldness, but I would wager a few of them do. If that describes you, then hello - let's hang out and lose hours talking about old movies.

The YouTube stuff and other content I create outside of excellent books like this one continue to serve that need I had when I discovered the scene and started writing about it - to ensure there is new content that appreciates these classic eras of cinema and media, to perpetuate and support a scene that was really good to me in the early days and continues to be good to me now.

I try to keep the videos to a certain length but I often get carried away if I find sellers online that have a particularly juicy inventory or something of particular note, like the other night when I found a copy of *Mutant Hunt* on eBay while filming and was ecstatic at seeing it in all of its tacky glory. The cover does kick ass, though. I love sharing my enthusiasm for it all and that's something that really keeps me going.

Back when I started my journey of discovery with the VHS scene and everything that came along with it, I realised I wasn't alone in this niche hobby I had and found a tribe that extended right around the globe. I was so grateful that I wanted to contribute to that scene and see it grow. Boom - ten years later there are hundreds of videos, articles, podcasts and further books full of me ranting about how great tapes were and are.

The thing is, there are loads of us around the world. Judging by my YouTube stats there are viewers in every continent. Even if they're not collectors, I bet they have similar stories to share of spending nights in video stores and discovering whole universes in those little plastic boxes of tape.

I see you, guys. I'm right there with you.

Chapter Fifteen
Trailer Compilations ate my brain

I have always loved movie trailers, be they on tape, disc, TV or the big screen. When they are done right, they're exciting, engrossing and entice you to see the full thing. When done wrong, they give away too much or show the film in a bad light. Either way, I adore them. I had the *Grindhouse* trailer DVD compilations and also loved the trailer discs on the two excellent *Video Nasties: The Definitive Guide* box sets and played the hell out of them.

I never skip trailers on VHS. They are sacred things that feel almost like tony films in their own right, adding further value to a purchase or a rental. There's something about them that I can't resist. The mystery of what they offer has always been exciting.

I'll even watch trailers for films I know off by heart and still get that trailer buzz from them. In fact, checking out trailers for much-loved movies often reveals things that didn't make it into the final cut of stuff, like alternate takes or entire scenes that don't show up in the finished product.

Something I'd wanted to do for ages was create some compilations of retro trailers that mixed genres and styles seemingly at random (albeit with a definite bias to horror and sci-fi movies). The intention was for it to play like trailers on a VHS tape, or evoke the experience of seeing loads of very different films vying for your attention on the video store racks we remember so fondly.

I found myself trawling the Internet Archive for trailers of all sorts; horror, sci-fi, action, comedy, dramas and whatever else popped up in searches. I gathered a crazy amount of them and edited them into three collections topped and tailed with new idents, music and some crackly TV static to set the mood properly. I was really pleased with them and would play them as background while writing or working or gaming or doing the dishes. They were oddly comforting.

I streamed each one live on my Twitch channel and spent each session chatting with other viewers about favourite films that would pop up in them or films they had forgotten about entirely. That was fun, but I wanted more.

I contacted my buddy Rob Lane from the 80s Video Shop and booked to screen the first collection on the big screen in their cinema room. I went along and had my own cinema party, which was awesome. I asked the 80s Video Shop guys to let anyone in if they wanted to join me, and a few did pop in and out of the screening. It was an interesting experience to see so many trailers that were familiar to me on a big screen rather than a TV screen. It made me wonder what it was like to see those trailers at the cinema for the first time. I do remember the thrill of seeing great trailers during cinema trips as a kid and a teenager, but not for any that I had included in these compilations.

I present here the lists of trailers that were included in each of the three volumes of the series, all made solely for fun.

THE VIDEO STORE ATE MY
BRAIN VOLUME 1

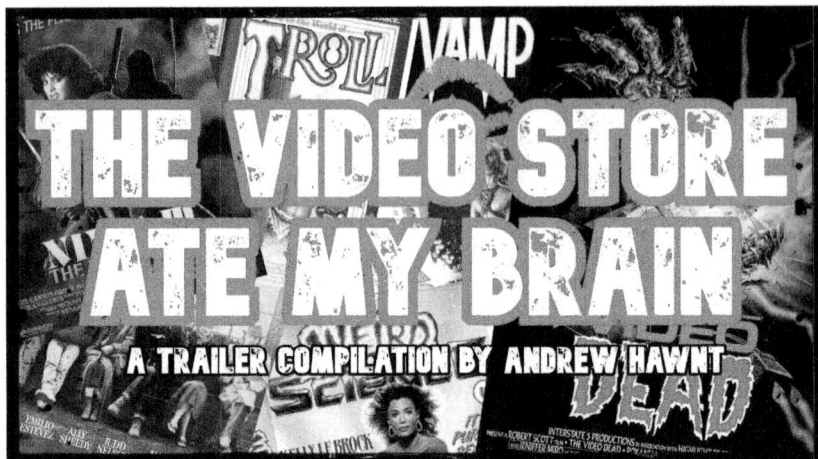

INTRO
VINTAGE 'PREVUES' CLIP
CLASS OF NUKE 'EM HIGH
FRIGHT NIGHT PART 2
A NIGHTMARE ON ELM STREET TV SPOT
SAVAGE STREETS
PLANES, TRAINS AND AUTOMOBILES
BASKET CASE
ST ELMO'S FIRE
NEMESIS
NINJA III: THE DOMINATION
VAMP

TRANCERS
THE GATE
THE VIDEO DEAD
BIG
CANNIBAL HOLOCAUST
RAGEWAR (aka THE DUNGEONMASTER)
ELIMINATORS
TRICK OR TREAT
TROLL
LIFEFORCE
RETURN OF THE LIVING DEAD III
MASTERS OF THE UNIVERSE
THE LAST STARFIGHTER
UNHOLY
WARRIOR OF THE LOST WORLD
CREEPOZOIDS
NIGHTBREED
SLAVE GIRLS FROM BEYOND INFINITY
GHOULIES
NEON MANIACS
EVIL DEAD

THE VIDEO STORE ATE MY BRAIN
VOLUME 2

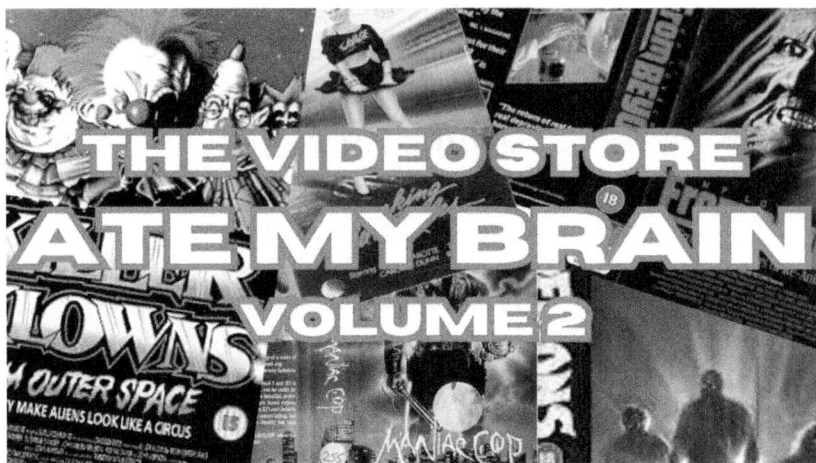

LADYHAWKE
HEAD OF THE FAMILY
THE SURE THING
SPACEHUNTER: ADVENTURES IN THE
FORBIDDEN ZONE
NO RETREAT, NO SURRENDER 3: BLOOD
BROTHERS
THE GREAT OUTDOORS
THE NINJA SQUAD
HALLOWEEN II
MANIAC COP
A NIGHTMARE ON ELM STREET 2: FREDDY'S
REVENGE
DEMONS
ESCAPE FROM NEW YORK
BREAKING ALL THE RULES
PSYCHIC KILLER
EXORCIST III
ELVIA - MISTRESS OF THE DARK
CONAN THE DESTROYER
GUARDIAN ANGEL
AMITYVILLE II: THE POSSESSION
AMERICAN NINJA III: BLOOD HUNT
PUPPET MASTER 2
LAST HOUSE ON THE LEFT

THE VIDEO STORE ATE MY BRAIN
VOLUME 3

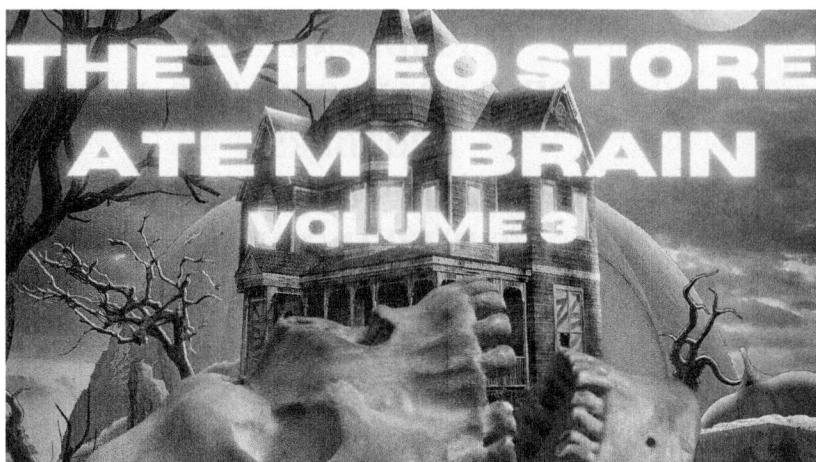

THE BEYOND
SUSPIRIA
THE NESTING
LADY TERMINATOR
GHOSTBUSTERS
THE BURNING
LIQUID SKY
BRONX WARRIORS
NIGHT LIFE
REPOSSESSED
HARDWARE
TROLL 2
THE WILLIES
DEATH MACHINE
BACK TO SCHOOL
RETURN OF THE LIVING DEAD
DAWN OF THE MUMMY
POLICE ACADEMY 3: BACK IN TRAINING
IRON EAGLE
TRON
THE DEADLY SPAWN
BARBARIAN QUEEN
THE THING

Chapter Sixteen
Launch night adventure

In keeping with a sequel to a book on nostalgia, I find myself coming full circle to a night that involved the first book, at least in its revised form.

When *VHS Ate My Brain: Revised Edition* was completed, Rob Lane of the 80s Video Shop and the Straight To Video Podcast dropped me a line to offer to host a launch event for it. That sounded like a dream come true, getting to launch the updated version of the book in the closest I would ever get to a real video rental store.

In that book I recounted a story where Rob had left me in charge of the shop for a few minutes, meaning I have, albeit briefly, run a video shop. Win! The place has become the epicentre of VHS appreciation for me, so kicking off the life of the new version of the book there made perfect sense.

I had a chunky batch of books sent to me that I could take along and had some custom bookmarks made. I packed them all into an oversized travel case and almost crippled myself getting them over to Alfreton. I already have issues walking properly thanks to my stupid ankle problems, so lugging the case onto trains and through the town once I got there was a long way from being the best idea I'd ever had.

Rob had gone all out with setting up for the night, which really meant a lot to me. He'd had posters printed advertising the night which were so cool to see. It was the first time I'd ever had posters made for anything I'd done and I loved seeing them as I came up to the shop before the night kicked off. The posters were also on the staircase and visible throughout the shop. That's when a new layer of nervousness crept up on me.

As with all things I create, I have a terrible feeling of imposter syndrome. This is unfounded as I'm honest in my content and want to be as real as I can. I really love this stuff, this weird little world of old movies, soundtracks, comics, books and t-shirts. It's a massive part of me, but still the imposter syndrome persists.

Rob and I set up the table with stacks of books, then also added rows of them to the VHS racks that line the shop. It turned out that, entirely by accident, the books fit perfectly on the racks, just like VHS tapes. That was satisfying. There were drinks and snacks, another screening of my first trailer compilation *The Video Store Ate My Brain* in the screening room and a live recording of an interview for both my Planet Hex channel and the 80s Video Shop channel.

Was it a huge night full of crowds and cheering? No, but I signed books for those that did show up and I'm hugely grateful to every one of them. Like the messages I still get from other countries, knowing that my daft book could lead to such a fun night in my favourite place filled me with pride.

We're not just antisocial film nerds lit only by the glow of CRT screens. We are legion.

Well, maybe not legion, but enough to fill a medium-sized room.

Rob gave me a lift back home afterwards, saving me a train journey and a taxi fare. We talked about movies, music and life, just like we always do when we're in the same place. Rob is someone who gets my thing about movies being markers along the story of your life. Many of us can remember when we first saw a favourite film, or maybe we remember a time when a particular film became a comfort blanket, as things like *The Breakfast Club, Trick Or Treat, A Nightmare on Elm Street 3: Dream Warriors* or *High Fidelity* have been for me. As soon as I think about those films they become page markers in my life story. *Trick or Treat?* I was 13 and deep into my early forays into being a metalhead kid. *Elm Street 3* was about the same time and ignited my lifelong love of Freddy Krueger as well as media that involves dreams, demons or both. *The Breakfast Club* was my go-to at about 15, with *Pretty in Pink* and other John Hughes movies close behind it.

I didn't see *High Fidelity (2000)* until maybe 2003 and found it at the point of my stupid 20s where I needed it most. Something about John Cusack's portrayal of Rob Gordon in that film really connected with me - his love of old media, old music, things that were tried and true, his penchant for dressing like an aged teenager and his pessimism.

(Side note - I didn't like the book that High Fidelity was based on anywhere near as much as the film, but the remake series starring Zoe Kravitz that came along in 2021 was really good. Shame it only lasted one series)

Rob listened to me go on (and on) about films and life with his customary patience and relentless good nature, sharing his own stories along the way. Funny how I associate the dude with another film marker, since I met him at a cinema screening of the VHS documentary *Adjust Your Tracking.*

I'm so grateful that those markers along the way are now embellished and enriched with like-minded people.

Interlude
Happy Happy Halloween

I was asked to guest on an episode of the *Silver Screen* podcast by a guy I know, Darren, who had not only worked in the same comic shop I had (before I started there though) but had also performed a role in my movie *The Demon and I*. The presenters were rounded out by writer Athena Williams.

We were tasked with discussing 1982's *Halloween III: Season of the Witch*, the infamous sequel that didn't feature Michael Myers at all and instead focused on killer masks being made by the strange Silver Shamrock company. It's an effective sci-fi-tinged horror movie that has a lot of memorable scenes but is often shunned by Michael Myers diehards. Well, dear Myers fans, Michael wasn't supposed to be the focus of the *Halloween* franchise. John Carpenter's original intention for the series was that each one should be a different story, creating a series of films that would play like feature-length episodes of *The Twilight Zone* or *The Outer Limits.* That isn't how things played out though, as Michael Myers and Laurie Strode proved to be such a hit that a sequel was quickly churned out that continued the story from the first, thus cementing Myers and Strode and Donald Pleasance's Dr Loomis as the core of the franchise.

As such, when this third movie came along, people were confused to be met with nary a moment of Myers (aside from a nod to the earlier films on TV in this one - very meta). This resulted in the film being lambasted for not being another stalk and slash cheapie and the series was canned until 1988 brought the Shape back in *Halloween 4:*

155

The Return of Michael Myers. Were audiences happy? Not really, and their distaste continued through *Halloween 5: The Revenge of Michael Myers (1989)* and the much-maligned *Halloween 6: The Curse of Michael Myers.* Things did eventually get back on track briefly with *Halloween H20* in the 90s, but that was followed with the dire *Halloween: Resurrection* which killed the franchise until Rob Zombie's ill-advised remakes and then the final trilogy with Jamie Lee Curtis returning, which are notable for ignoring pretty much all of the franchise.

But anyway, as the podcast unfolded over almost two hours of chat, it became increasingly obvious that *Halloween III* wasn't a bad film at all, rather just misunderstood and underappreciated because of the Myers legacy. It definitely had an audience, and while there were no William Shatner masks painted white in the Silver Shamrock range, the film has a lot of memorable and potentially iconic scenes, such as the repeated and decidedly creepy 'Happy happy Halloween' theme tune played over and over on TV, enticing kids to wear their masks on Halloween so the evil could be spread as far as possible. The eventual attack from the masks is grisly and horrific, and its ambiguous ending adds a few notches to the tension. Did they stop the evil influence of Silver Shamrock? We'll never know thanks to that silent arsehole Michael Myers coming back and ruining any chances of an interesting franchise unfolding.

It was a pleasure to go on the show and I look forward to guesting again* as there's nothing quite like sitting down with like-minded people and just offloading all of the trivia you've been saving up for special occasions.

156

(*I did guest again, covering the insane video-era flick *Waxwork,* and again I had a blast)

Chapter Seventeen
VHS Content creators on the last ten years

There are a lot of content creators out there making nostalgic content that celebrates and examines the VHS era and all that went along with it, and I really admire them for doing so. It all helps to catalogue these things and ensure that new generations know what happened, and that they know we were there and lived it ourselves.

Gareth Packham (Video Tasties)

The Video Tasties YouTube channel is a paradise for the vintage film nerd. There are watch parties, discussions, interviews and many, many other videos, all made by the one and only Gareth Packham, a man with more tapes in his house than is healthy. But hey, we're Tapeheads, and we love what we love. How long has the Video Tasties thing been rolling along?

"Must be two and a half years now," he tells me in his typically calm manner. Gareth is quite a low-key individual until you get him onto the subject of films. This is easy, thankfully.

As an active collector and content creator, how do you think the VHS and retro film community has evolved over the past decade?

"There has definitely been a resurgence, but as with anything like this it goes up and down in terms of interest. And like you show on your YouTube channel, you see the prices fluctuate. It used to be that some films would go for a pound on eBay and yet now they're being priced at fifty quid for the same thing. Who's buying that? They were so much cheaper before. They were 10 A penny back in the day."

You're not kidding. In the video I did this week I saw two copies of *Hardware* (the 1990 dystopian sci-fi flick). One was like 70 pounds and one was 60. it's crazy, as the copy I have cost me a pound or so. I wondered if it was just *Hardware*, but a lot of tapes are skyrocketing in price lately.

"I can understand it when actors die that people get sentimental and pick up their VHS tapes and stuff, but it's still a surprise. Like with Carl Weathers recently. I got an ex-rental copy of *Action Jackson* for ten pounds last week and it's already gone up in price. It's an entertaining film, not a great one, but the price has clearly been hiked up because he passed away."

Do you think the scene is less niche now? Do you see an audience from around the world in your analytics?

"Mostly UK and America – some in South America. Those are mainly the areas that get my humour."

Do you think we are headed for a vinyl-type situation with VHS?

"In some ways, yes. I started collecting again 4 or 5 years ago. I saw on eBay the *Star Wars* trilogy, the ones in the blue

159

covers, rereleased about 25 years ago (laughs). I thought they'd be nice to have and it just snowballed from there."

I totally understand that. What keeps you interested in creating content on vintage films?

"I don't know (laughs)."

Gareth picks up a nearby copy of *The Untouchables*.

"Take this for example. The first time I saw *The Untouchables*, I saw it on VHS. The same cover as this. It was an important one for me. I fell in love with that film, even though it was a terrible pan-and-scan fullscreen copy. I guess preservation and appreciation are the main things."

Oh man, pan and scan… I don't miss that.

"Yeah. There's a bit in the film when Elliot Ness is coming home and Frank is outside his house and they're talking about his daughter. And then Elliot runs into the house and runs upstairs, where he finds the bed with his daughter on it. On the Pan and Scan version, you just see the corner of the bed and it clearly zips over to show where she is – it's quite jarring."

It was good when widescreen releases started showing up on VHS.

"I agree. I collected quite a lot of widescreen tapes as I thought, 'this is how it's supposed to be seen'. Like the *Star Wars* widescreen VHS set I mentioned. It was like seeing a different film! I guess 4:3 pan and scan did mean that you got more 'open matte', more top and bottom of the image – and more boom mics and nudity in the shot! (laughs)"

'Booms mics and nudity' sounds like a Troma film. What do you think lies in store for the future of the scene?

"I don't know, because... Vinyl is different as you can still easily buy a record player. You can't easily find a VHS player.

I have three so I have backups. Sometimes a charity shop will have them, sometimes they don't. It's hard to pick one up so that limits things straight away."

With the popularity of *Stranger Things* and other retro stylised media, do you think that a younger generation will be introduced to a lot of vintage films? How do you think they'd react? I mean, they'll be aware of things like *The Godfather*, but imagine sitting them down for an Andy Sidaris marathon or some Troma movies. They would wonder what the hell was happening.

"They would be in for a treat (laughs)!"

They'd think we were all weird in the past.

"Most people think I'm weird anyway!"

I hear you, man.

"I think what they would find weird is the idea of going out to a shop in order to rent a film, watch it once or twice and take it back. That was half the fun. The aisles of tapes."

And of course tapes, DVDs and Blu-rays don't get deleted from your library, unlike streaming services and their unpredictable culls.

"Yes! I've recently been revisiting *Parks and Rec* and went to start the next episode and the whole series was pulled in front of me. I was aghast. I've never found a film on Netflix that I wanted to see that they didn't make. No matter what I search for on there, they don't have it."

What's your favourite VHS-related thing recently? Mine has to be my many visits to the 80s Video Shop.

"You git! (laughs) I still need to go. I guess for me it's the thrill of finding something I haven't seen before. I just got *King of the Kickboxers* and it's epic. I loved it. It's like *Bloodsport* crossed with *Kickboxer* on steroids. Crazy shit."

161

Crazy shit is what we like, man.

The Loft Movie Theatre (Lucy and Gavin)

The Loft Movie Theatre is a film club that screens vintage movies, often at the wonderful Savoy cinema in Nottingham. Whether the film is *Die Hard, The Crow, Big Trouble in Little China* or any of the others they have brought back to the big screen at their events, they know their crowd and they know how to entertain. Run by film addicts Lucy and Gavin, they're an integral part of the local retro scene.

I was at the screening of *Return of the Living Dead* and both the turnout and the audience reception were superb. What do you think is the beating heart of the expansion of the vintage film fan scene over the last ten years?

"In the 70s, 80s and even into the 90s, going to see a new film was a real event. There was a sense of mass anticipation with a film being advertised to the whole population in trailers, on TV and in newspapers. Then going to the cinema felt exciting – you'd come out feeling like you'd had an experience! And if you didn't go and see it again at the cinema, there weren't many ways you could

162

revisit it - especially not until the advent of home video. So, if you really loved a film, you'd hanker after everything about it. You'd talk about it with friends, you might have posters or toys, and if you found a small 'behind the scenes' article in a magazine, you'd pore over every word."

I miss doing that!

"But the way we consume media these days is totally different. We have this grazing culture where there's so much content out there, and everything is here today gone tomorrow, so it's impossible to get excited about a new film in the same way – as a person or as a collective audience. So, for people around our age, seeing a film from that era on the big screen, and especially with a like-minded audience - can transport us back and give us a bit of that feeling of excitement and connection once again."

The glow of familiarity is intoxicating.

"Nostalgia is a very powerful thing – it makes us feel a sense of comfort amidst the complexities of adulthood and the modern world. You can see how the film industry cashes in on this with the release of 'nostalgia bait' fan service films like the recent *Ghostbusters* sequels. But for us, and many like us, films like that will never have the magic or originality of some of our favourites from our formative years."

So what would you say are sequels that recapture the power of the originals - or build on them?

"*Aliens* and *Terminator 2: Judgement Day* are both great examples of sequels where the initial film has been expanded upon and amped up to the next level, but where the heart of the story and the characterisation have not been lost along the way - which can sometimes happen with sequels. *Mad Max* is a weird one because the first film is so far removed from the rest. Each subsequent film is really just a retelling – but the experience intensifies through incremental worldbuilding. *Mad Max 2* is fantastic - that was one of our favourite Loft Movie Theatre screenings last year – and *Mad Max Fury Road* is one of our favourite films of the last ten years."

I'm of the same opinion. *Fury Road* is a beast. See you at the cinema!

Chris Annable (GluBob Productions/80s Video Shop)

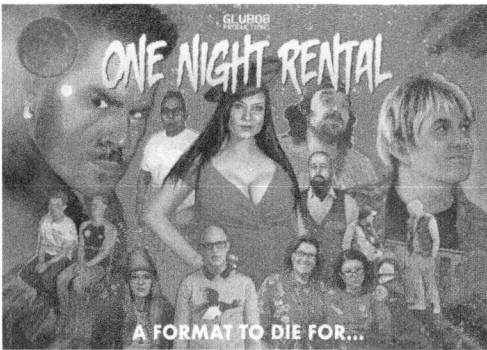

Chris isn't just a nice bloke with a wry sense of humour and a ridiculous amount of film knowledge. He's also one of the guys behind my favourite place in the world, the 80s Video Shop in Alfreton. Now he has another awesome claim to fame as director of *One Night Rental*, a nerdy, View Askiewniverse-style comedy set in, of course, the 80s Video Shop itself. It must be an amazing feeling to see your work - and the shop - on the big screen like you did at the recent cinema premiere!

"Thank you – I get bored quite easily and keep doing stupid things! Maybe I'll try out swimming in the Olympics next."

So is *One Night Rental* your first time making a movie?

"I've always had the idea to do something like this. I used to write scripts at university. I had a camcorder when I was about 15 and me and my mates tried to make a film and found out it's not as straightforward as you think. I was always massively into film and in a weird way I like the making of films rather than the films themselves a lot of the time. I love commentaries and that sort of stuff. Then I have to surround myself with people with the patience to make things. I mean, I can think of things and write them down, but as far as editing and messing about with clapper boards, I can't focus. I just want to put together a story. If I knew it was as hard as this (*One Night Rental*) I probably wouldn't have done it (laughs). I'm going to do it again though (laughs)."

So now via your GluBob Productions turning the 80s Video Shop into a movie location and more films coming, are we going to – wait for the pun – see a shared GLUniverse onscreen?

"You couldn't help yourself, could you?"

No. Tee hee.

"That'd be awesome! I haven't thought about it to be honest, but potentially (laughs). All these films are kind of roughly planned out. The first one is set in the shop. The second is also set in the shop but not as much, and then the third one planned is away from the shop. They're standalone stories but also interconnected. The shop is an amazing setting, but I didn't want to just retread old ground each time."

Great idea to do the first one there though, I mean you have an instant location with the different rooms and stuff, all self-contained and shut off from distractions.

"Yeah, that helped massively. I mean, proper directors have been in the shop who've made films with millions in the budget and they've said it would have cost so, so much to make as a film set, so that was brilliant. It's kind of why I wanted to do it as we had a set ready built. It's self-contained and looks great. We didn't need to recreate anything."

The shop has been open for 18 months or so now. How has it been received by visitors?

"Amazingly well. People really like it. Nobody has come in and gone 'Well, this is pointless.' The response has been phenomenal. We originally said we'd try it for a month. Just a month to see how it went, but it's been insane. We don't take it for granted, but it has been an amazing response. People who get it *really* get it. It's a little bit niche, but not that much as so many people remember going to the video shop."

You and Rob (Lane) did a brilliant job making it, man.

"Rob's probably the more polished version of me. I just come up with the crazy idea and Rob moulds it. My own version would have been nowhere near as good as what we've got."

Why do you think the retro scene has grown so much in the last decade? Is it just that old nerds have a bit more money now?

"You might be right there, mate (laughs). People have got into their 40s and early 50s and want to revisit something that was around in their youth, something that's not accessible any more. Nostalgia is a huge thing. It gives a buzz. A good feeling. If I see something that reminds me of being a kid, say an advert about *Batman*, I'm taken back to being a kid in 1989, Christmas. When things were easier.. So few people collect physical things now, so a physical store is like a time capsule or a museum, and it reminds you that, you know what? It was *shit hot* at the time. It was brilliant. It was about getting stuff you really wanted or discovering something you didn't expect. Nobody seems to have the patience now. There's just that much stuff around now it's hard to get excited about a lot of it."

And streaming services just take stuff down.

"It's scary. I've had things I paid for just vanish from services. Maybe people will get tired of it being like this and go back to more physical media, I don't know, but people may moan about plastics or something. I think most of it comes down to a lot of people being too busy doing nothing to go out and seek out something exciting. It's a shame. We've kind of created a society of people who are condemned to their homes. You can order food, get films, it's a bit scary and I believe it contributes to everyone's low moods."

I do miss the video store I spent so much time in. Just being there, surrounded by it all, was fun. Whereas when you watch streaming, you often get the same sort of thing advertised to you and you may end up limiting your own awareness.

"That's absolutely true. They point you in a certain direction, taking away freedom of choice in some respects., I know what you mean about the feeling about going into places. There was a place near me called Circle-K and even though there was only a couple of racks of tapes there it was heaven for me. I'd go there and probably end up picking *Die Hard* for the 50th time (laughs). Not to sound like an old git, but things were, to me, better then. There was anticipation and excitement over things that has just all gone now. I used to get my videos out at home, this may seem a bit sad, but I'd get them out and people would come round to our house in my village to rent videos from my house. It was great. I had about 200 tapes. I used to rate the tapes, spine, back, front, I'd rate them out of ten. Inevitable really that the shop would eventually exist."

Dreams do come true I guess!

Rob Lane (Straight to Video/80s Video Shop/Actor in *One Night Rental*)
(Photo by Scott Cole)

Rob is one of my favourite people in the world. A wildly talented bassist, the man behind the Straight to Video brand that encompasses an incredible podcast packed with great guests, a range of merchandise, YouTube videos, albums and, alongside previous interviewee Chris Annable, the 80s Video Shop in Alfreton. Rob is my longest-serving friend in the retro community and is a genuine, decent guy with hair and looks that I am deeply envious of. It's a good job he's such a cool person.

168

It has been quite a busy decade since his previous interview in the first *VHS Ate My Brain*. Heck, it's been crazy just since *VHS Ate My Brain: Revised Edition* was launched in the shop nine months before this sequel, what with there being an actual feature film shot in the shop, starring Rob himself in one of the lead roles.

"I can't believe it's been ten years since you did the first *VHS Ate My Brain*. That's about as long as we've known each other, isn't it?"

Yeah, we met first at the screening of VHS documentary *Adjust Your Tracking* that you did at Screen 22.

"It's so cool that it was that one. I don't think there were many people there for that one."

I still have the flyer for it somewhere. Great night. I remember there was cake.

"That was the kick-start for a lot of things. How did you hear about the screening?"

I think it was through the *Horror VHS Collectors Unite* page on Facebook. I think Dan Kinem (*Adjust Your Tracking*'s director) or someone posted about it. I was delighted it was here and not thousands of miles away like all the other stuff that was on the group at the time. So much has changed since those days. And here we are with you running a video store. What has the experience of running the 80s Video Shop taught you about the perception of the video rental era?

"I think the main thing that I've come across is that everyone has the same story and I never get bored of hearing it. They always tell us, 'This is amazing, I used to spend so long picking out films in the video shop with my mum or my dad'. It still resonates and that was the goal

169

when we set up the shop. If nothing else, we've achieved the goal with that. I think the main thing I've discovered when meeting proper diehard VHS fans like yourself is that I don't know shit about it (laughs)"

I'd say you know loads about several parts of it, say stuff like *Licence To Drive* and that sort of teen action comedy-drama, but no matter how long you go through it there's always something new to find. I had that the other night when I found *Smithereens*. Never heard of it before and really liked it.

"I know, right? You feel so dumb! But that's the thing – with VHS shops in particular, you saw the poster there and you thought that film was the biggest thing around. You expected everybody else to have seen that poster and know that's a massive film. But nowadays you mention a lot of old titles and people have never even heard of them."

They were big to you, though, and that matters. Because they had posters, it must have been good!

"Totally, and you don't realise what an impression they made on you at the time, and it holds true today. It's an ongoing journey of learning. It's always fun to meet people and speak to them. I love it that there's so much to take in. I was watching one of your videos the other day and you brought up *Mutant Hunt* for example. I've never even heard of it."

Yeah, *Mutant Hunt* is crazy. The cover is amazing, but the film is… a bit of a chore, but fun. It's one of those Empire movies that started life as a poster and the poster was given to the film-makers in order to make something that looked like it!

"Quality (laughs). Another one to add to the list."

170

Does everyone have the same reaction when they walk into the shop for the first time?

"Some do. Usually they ask how it works – do we rent the tapes? Do people still have players? I had a family in at the weekend, a dad and his wife and kid. He was by far the most excited. He loved it. You could see the memories were all resurfacing."

Probably all the memories of being in the video shop with mum or dad, figuring out what to watch before going home for chips, like many of my early video store memories. Congratulations on passing 18 months of the shop by the way. Chris (Annable) was saying that the original idea was to only open it for a month.

"Yeah, one of my original pitches to Chris was doing it as a pop-up shop. He was like, no, no. Let's give it a shot."

So from your perspective, after doing the movie nights, the music, the t-shirts, the shop and now a movie, where do you see this scene going next?

"It's a bit of unknown territory, really I think. Obviously, the 80s have stayed popular. They say everything has like a 30-year cycle, but the 80s nostalgia is really holding in there (laughs). The 90s are becoming more popular now as well, so still very VHS and video shop-related. I don't know how much VHS can creep back. Probably not as much as vinyl. I think more films will be released on tape again, so I think it'll be good for creatives. Someone said they wondered if we would see actual video players show up in shops again. That would be a huge thing to do but I don't know who would be willing to do it. It's not like trying to reissue the Walkman or something. Anyone who has opened up a video player will understand how insane they are inside and have no idea how they work. I don't! (laughs)"

It's like witchcraft in there. I think maybe the aesthetic will last a while rather than tapes coming back in a big way. I mean, tapes will always be bought and sold and traded among the diehards that grew up with them, but I think things like apps that give videos the old look, retro fashions and art styles will outlast the wider awareness of the VHS scene.

"Yeah, t-shirts, apparel, logos. I'd say that's how it will continue outside the scene."

So, after ten years since I interviewed you for the first *VHS Ate My Brain*, do you still have the love for tapes, the films, the whole shebang?

"Yes. I still love it, man. There's still that magic there. Even just walking into the shop we created, there's still a buzz when I go in. I do miss being able to go into a charity shop and buy a stack of ex-rentals for next to nothing, though! I remember when I used to buy loads of them and dump the covers and tapes just so I could release the next STV thing in a tape case! That's how common they were. I was just buying stuff and throwing it away. It's a crazy thought now."

I see a few in three or four charity shops these days, but only occasionally.

"Do you think they've all been dumped?"

Yeah, actually. I've actually seen it – round the back of a row of shops here there's a car park I sometimes use, and one day I was there and spotted a skip outside the back of the Barnardo's we used to have here. It was full of VHS and cassettes, all ruined by rain. It was heartbreaking. Everyone moved on, but everything is cyclic like you said. I'm just glad – and really grateful – that people like you and Chris and others out there are doing what you do.

"I think with it becoming more current and mainstream again, you've probably witnessed this, I think some collectors may have been put off by the new enthusiasts. Whether you could say they're gatekeeping or not I don't know. You can't stop it though. Just embrace it. There's things like the grading of tapes which I find a bit weird."

I don't want to be a gatekeeper with this stuff. As long as someone is enjoying the films rather than just buying them to have as a paperweight or a bit of kitsch, I say the more the merrier.

"There's so much to learn and so much history. It's always fun. I just wish I had the brain capacity to remember everything that people tell me! (laughs)"

Well please do keep it up with the shop, the music and that excellent podcast. In closing, as this is a sequel, what's your favourite follow-up?

"(Laughs) Have I got to nail it down to one?"

Nah man, maybe one per genre or something. Let's get nuts.

"I think the standout one for me has to be *Aliens*. My standout sequel. I was lucky enough to see that at the cinema in America, where it was rated R so I could get in as long as I had an adult with me (laughs). I was about 11 and it terrified me, but it still stands up. The teaser trailer for it is a masterpiece as well. A couple of others I love would be *Beverly Hills Cop 2*, which often gets overlooked, but I love it. It's peak Eddie Murphy. *Gremlins 2* as well. That was like 'There's no way we can top the original film. Let's just do whatever the hell we want – and it worked! It's chaotic and anarchic and brilliant. *Lethal Weapon 2* is another great one. *Back to the Future 2* has a perfect ending. If it had to be just one I would go with *Aliens*."

Thanks for taking part in this crazy thing, dude. I wish I was as cool as you.

Josh Schafer (Lunchmeat VHS)

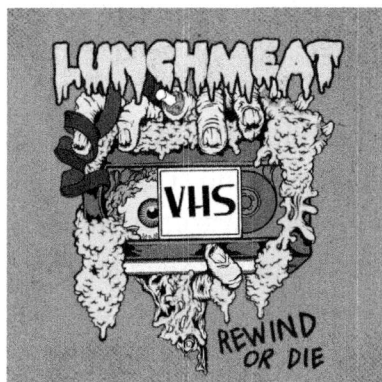

Josh Schafer is a genuine VHS scene legend. Based in the States, he is the mastermind behind Lunchmeat VHS, which offers VHS-inspired apparel, movies on tape, a wide variety of zines and merch and of course the excellent Lunchmeat VHS magazine. He's one of the guiding lights of the scene and a bit of a hero of mine, which is why it blew my mind when he offered to design the cover of the original *VHS Ate My Brain* after he'd seen my abysmal original attempt. I 100% believe that his artwork was instrumental in getting a lot of people to notice that book and I'll always be grateful for that.

What else should you know about Josh? He doesn't age. He's almost sickeningly handsome, talented and sweet. His enthusiasm and creativity are infectious, and I do believe that without his input we wouldn't have such a vibrant VHS scene now.

So yeah, thank you!

"No problem man, it's so good to speak to you! I feel like we've known each other forever!"

So a decade on from all the stuff we saw growing when I did the first book, how have you seen the scene evolve?

"It's incredible. I mean it's truly incredible, like I would have never imagined it would get this big, you know? It's everywhere now, I mean, it's really hard to articulate, I just see it everywhere now. There's like there's so many people doing VHS tapes, whether they're official or special edition limited runs or bootlegging, trying to you know just make their own art, it really feels that to a certain level, VHS is back. The aesthetic, the nostalgia, everything. I love it."

Something I'm really pleased about is that it doesn't seem to be made fun of or belittled for being old school. I worried that when it gained a greater awareness in the public eye outside of the scene it would be seen as a bit silly.

"No man, it's the opposite. People loved video stores, loved choosing tapes and having that whole experience with friends and family or whoever. It was cool and that shared nostalgia hits home in a big way."

You have to admit you've played a big part in that nostalgia, though. You really put the love of tapes on the map with Lunchmeat.

"Thanks bro, I mean I do what I can. I just do what I'm passionate about and I'm just really thankful that the Lunchmeat platform has been so well received and people enjoy it you know, but to pick up on what you said, you know I think there are still people that make fun of it but I mean who gives a shit? Who gives a *VHshit* what they think, you know what I mean? (laughs)"

I certainly do.

"It's not for everybody and that's I think that's part of the surprise to me is how big of a fandom there is. You and I know it makes sense, because of the huge part of our culture and a huge part of media progress and a huge part of communication in general that is the videotape, right? You know, your work, my work, countless others' work has brought it to a lot of people and made them think about it together, you know to rewind back to those times and say hey, you know, that was really fun! I think that's what it's about. It's about having fun, like the 'VHS is happiness' slogan."

I should have worn my VHS is Happeness shirt to talk to you! Tapes do seem to bring a smile to peoples' faces when they remember the video store years.

"It's incredible, dude. I mean I've met so many great people through Lunchmeat and you know, something that I started in my early 20s as just like a passion project has become my career. It's been really fun, wild, and incredible to be able to contribute the way I have and for people to collaborate with. It's been amazing man."

It's funny, but when I wrote the first of these books I felt kind of alone here in the UK as the *Horror VHS Collectors Unite* page and other groups had me believing that it was primarily a US scene, but then I found Rob Lane and people like that and found there was much more interest here than I had expected. I figured it was a niche thing that would only appeal to me, so finding other people was mindblowing. What is that it keeps you engaged with VHS and the scene after after all these years?

"I think really it's seeing the community and the culture grow. It's seeing the enthusiasm and it kind of like bounces back at you right? I've given out so much enthusiasm and passion over the past 15 years I think seeing it come back to you and seeing people just write you letters or notes and say thank you for what you do for the community and the culture... it's really invigorating."

Yeah, that energy exchange keeps it fun.

"That's what makes me feel good about what I'm doing, also just personally like I still love it. I still watch tapes every day. I still look for tapes all the time you know. It's my lifestyle. I watch streaming just like everybody else if there's something that I want to see and streaming, but I have a VCR in every room you know (laughs). Honestly man like I'm still discovering stuff every day you know whether it's new movies or old movies and you know it's there's so much discovery and history just embedded in the VHS format and it'll never stop. I really believe that it'll continue to grow and then we'll continue to find things and find new reasons to love VHS and what it's done."

I like to think how I know a fair bit about old movies but I'm still finding stuff I've never heard of and that's really exciting, even just to see another snapshot of an era that I've not seen since I was a kid. In closing, community is a big factor in VHS collecting as we've discussed. How would you describe the community to someone just discovering it what would you think they would be in store for?

"Oh man, a lot of information, a lot of enthusiasm and a lot of photographs of cool collections. A lot of creativity. It's a whole universe, constantly expanding. You're constantly meeting new people, you're constantly seeing new people enter that universe, but what's in store for them? Movies man, great artwork, a lot of fun. Of course, there are trolls everywhere, that's the internet in 2024 and is what we deal with, right, but overall the VHS community I think it's

177

something that you make acquaintances, friends, colleagues. The connective tissue is your appreciation for these movies because that's how a lot of us discovered them and then we reminisce about that, but then we also talk about their relevance to today's culture. It is just a huge conversation that's constantly swirling and swirling and new ideas are coming from it, new art forms are coming from it. It's fun and informative. If you hop into the community, you're going to make some friends you're gonna find out about new movies and you're gonna have a lot of fun."

And that's what keeps it all alive. Long live Lunchmeat and long live this crazy scene.

Visit Josh's Lunchmeat sit at www.lunchmeatvhs.com

Finale
Life is a movie

It's probably a lifetime of 90-minute adventures having an effect on my addled brain more than anything else, but I am, to a certain extent, of the opinion that life is like a movie. Your early years are the opening titles and the setup. You get to know the characters and the mechanics of the piece through the first act, then suddenly you find yourself in the conflict and character arcs of the second act before you head for an epic third act before, inevitably, the credits roll on your time on Earth.

Along the way you meet friends, you make mistakes, you have your regrets and your dreams and you fight every step of the way to get the ending that you dream of. Some people get there in great style with a third act of explosions, special effects and a cast of thousands.

Others move into that third act in a quieter fashion, thoughtful and humble in nature but no less fulfilling. It's all down to the writer and director to figure out which sort of third act you're in for. As the writer and director yourself, you have the right and the tools to try and make the finished product come out the way you wanted it to. Some can pull it off, but those people are either lucky, rich or have more energy than me.

Here in the midst of middle age, I hope my own third act is a long way off yet, but I'm doing my best to make sure it's a good one for me and those I love.

Nostalgia is a big part of my life, but the past isn't somewhere I want to live. Not yet anyway. I maintain that films are markers along the way. Like old photos or a mix CD you found at the back of a wardrobe. Snapshots of times lived through and, not lost, but moved on from. Fashions. Hairstyles (well, not in my case as I've been bald since my early twenties). Decor. The old car. It all tells you a story of where you were and who you were at any given moment along the way.

Now these books do this for me as well. Life was very different ten years ago, or a little longer ago while I was first writing material for what would become the original book. We have lost people along the way. We have experienced joy and sadness and depression and delight and hardship and enough good times to balance the bad. I remember them all, and whenever I go through my film library I see things that were there with me every step of the way, movies that took me away from situations that were driving me mad, even just for 90 minutes. Those movies are my heroes. In many ways, those movies saved my sanity and, probably, my life.

All of which is really bloody deep for a book about VHS tapes. The thing is, the tapes have been with me at my worst and at my best and aside from some tracking issues or the occasional chewed-up film, they've never let me down. Tapes have been there as solace, a safe space and a source of income over the years. Little boxes of magnetic tape that captured my imagination as a child have given me so much in return for buying them.

They gave me the impetus to write the first *VHS Ate My Brain*, the *VHS Ate My Brain* magazine column that followed it, the short-lived *VHS Ate My Brain* podcast, the eventual *VHS Ate My Brain: Revised Edition* and this sequel you're reading. Tapes brought me things I didn't expect, such as a circle of weird but brilliant friends, messages from all over the world, a little exposure for my writing career and a lot of great nights in front of various TVs.

Knowing that there are people out there all over the world collecting and watching and preserving tapes is amazing. Knowing there are companies like Shout Factory, Vinegar Syndrome, 101 Films, Arrow Video and many others putting out video-era movies on Blu-Ray is reassuring, as even if the tapes get mouldy and damp and are lost to time, that crazy era of cinema will be kept alive in some way.

A side effect of being known for my love of tapes is that friends and family will pass things on to me. Most recently an awesome friend called Pip turned up at the house with two boxes of VHS for me that he was throwing out. Pip was one of many great people I met while enduring a shitty job in a comic shop that should have been so much better. The place was terrible, as were the pay and the late closing, but I did emerge after nine years there with some great friends who have really stood the test of time.

Pip is one of those dudes you just pick up where you left off with, like no time had passed. He had brought his old collection over for me to go through, and it was a delight.

The boxes were full of mass-market tapes and stuff recorded off the TV, but it was treasure to me, knowing full well that a bunch of those tapes had got Pip through long nights just as my tapes had done for me.

A couple of days ago I attended an event that once again brought home that I am not alone in this niche of people who remember videos being a big part of our lives. The 80s Video Shop celebrated its 2nd anniversary. Following my interviews with Rob and Chris from the shop, it was wonderful to see the place make it two years into their journey. How long the place will run is anyone's guess, but two years existing as a video store museum, escape room, cinema room and retro bedroom attraction is a hell of an achievement, especially considering there's no entrance fee or anything to go along and hang out there.

I was tired, my ankles were hurting and it was far too hot for my Yorkshire-born disposition, but I wanted to be there.

I wanted to spend a little time there and recharge my batteries a bit. So I caught a train over to Alfreton yet again.

There were attractions, namely movie poster artist Paul Shipper would be there, plus YouTuber Jack Horrorhound and his demented puppet Galvaston. There was a raffle, a screening, even cakes offered. The moment I arrived I was greeted by Chris Annable along with two of his actors from *One Night Rental*, namely Rick Mallin and Neil 'Nidge' Green. Rick is also known for the *Old AF Reviewers* YouTube channel. Rick was a creepy bastard in the film and so it was entertaining to see how lovely he is to talk to. The same with Nidge, who was a delight too.

I headed upstairs, taking in the freshly redecorated staircase walls which had just been recovered with VHS covers. As I went up, I hoped that others had turned up. I wanted the event to be a hit for Rob and Chris as well as the community.

I need not have worried. The place was the busiest I've ever seen, people crowded in all over the place, chatting, checking out tapes, meeting Paul Shipper and exploring the place. People were playing video games, laughing and nerding out. Rob and Chris were surrounded by friends and fans, all there to celebrate the secret little oasis they had built.

I hung out with Paul for a while and found out he knew my old buddy, superstar artist Matt Ferguson. Paul asked me to sign his copy of *VHS Ate My Brain: Revised Edition*, which was so nice of him. I chatted with Rob and Chris, Jack Horrorhound and Galvaston the demon puppet. I caught up with friends, made some new ones and even ran into Midnite City frontman Rob Wylde, which was weird as I'd been listening to his band on the way there. I picked up *Batman* and *Robocop* prints from Paul, then headed to the cinema room to sit and watch the second half of *Back to the Future*, which I've never seen on the big screen before. I spent some time filming for my channel and tried to soak up everything I could from the day. That's something I do love about making videos for YouTube - getting to capture a little bit of what makes some days so special.

I left there happy, pleased at such a good turnout for Rob and Chris, but also that a weird little place full of retro gear and old VHS tapes could bring in such a crowd. The scene is full of people who genuinely love these things, and that is such a pleasure for me as an enthusiast and a content creator. We're out there.

This is also in evidence in the groups online, even now, long past those strange but exciting early days of places like *Horror VHS Collectors Unite*.

It brings a warm glow of excitement - and jealousy - when I see the amazing home video store setups that enthusiasts near and far have put so much love into. The collections that make my diminished stash look even smaller. Same with the events that take place in various countries that bring people together in the name of old movies on a dead format. Just brilliant. It's incredible to think that, ten years on from writing a book that I thought nobody would read, fans are still talking about tapes and sitting down to watch films that predate the internet.

Knowing that I have been a small part of the evolution of the scene over the past decade is a weird but beautiful thing. I didn't do any of this to make money or gain status. I mean, if I wanted to do that I wouldn't have written about

184

VHS! I did this to give something back, to take part in a scene that is spread across the world and isn't always accessible to me.

What have the books and other things I've done brought me? They brought me a lot of unexpected friends both near and far, as well as the joy of finding out that my knowledge about VHS tapes and old-school films is just the tip of a gigantic iceberg. I keep being introduced to titles I've never even heard of, let alone seen. It's amazing to me that so far in the future after the heights of the video era, there is still so much left to discover and enjoy.

Life has been a strange ride since my first rentals blew my mind with images of Freddy Krueger, Sammi Curr, Belial and Romero's zombies. My twenties were weird and broken. My thirties felt like I was making up for lost time and my forties - so far - feel like I'm finally getting a handle on who I am.

All of the pop culture stuff I have written over the years has an autobiographical element to it, because the pop culture intake of our youth has a profound effect on us as we grow. It certainly did for me. I use writing as therapy, as I can't bring myself to ever have an actual therapist. I don't want to talk about things unless it's with someone who gets where I'm coming from. People who get my pop culture references, my fascination with films and my endless enjoyment and appreciation of VHS tapes and the culture surrounding them.

So people like you, really.

Thanks for joining me for my sequel. Thanks for being there while I talk about tapes and how they're woven through my life.

Mainly, thanks for hanging out.

Don't forget to rewind.

***

The villains have been vanquished. The day has been saved. The heroes strode defiantly away from the final explosion, silhouetted against its blazing fury. The epilogue has played out. The screen fades to black and a kickass song starts up as the credits roll. You watch them all the way through the cast and crew, the Best Boy, the Gaffer, the Key Grip and all the rest. You feel that it's only fair to do so as they worked so hard to put the film together. You wonder what else they worked on and idly make a mental note to look some of them up. Especially the effects crew, as you've found some great stuff that way when you looked up KNB effects, Kevin Yagher and, of course, the legendary Tom Savini.

You note down your favourite songs you heard in the film and who performed them. Maybe you can find the soundtrack album or maybe releases with those individual artists, as you did with Dokken and their 'Back For the Attack' album because you wanted the 'Dream Warriors' song from A Nightmare on Elm Street Part 3: Dream Warriors. Thankfully the rest of the album was great as well, especially 'Kiss of Death' and 'Mr Scary'.

Maybe there's a cheap copy of the film on the market stalls you visit. You'll check them at the weekend as this was a pretty good flick.

The credits come to their end and the music fades out. You stop the tape and set it rewinding, satisfied with your rental and eager to make sure the video store people don't get annoyed with you when you take the tape back. It's your favourite place apart from bed and the comic shop you like in town and you want to keep them happy. Not just because they've got your name on two posters for when they reach the end of their advertising period, but because you like them and, if you're honest, you wish you were like them. You would love to spend your days behind the counter at the video store, renting out tapes and displaying new releases and helping film fans get their fix, but you never ask about a job there. In an odd way, you have raised those shop workers up to be celebrities in your mind. The coolest people in town.

The tape finishes rewinding and you put it back in the rental case, making sure to do it so the tape is the right way round and the clamshell clicks safely shut.

You clear the snack wrappers and empty drinks cans away. The noise on the streets outside has faded. The back-to-back films have done their trick and taken you away from your worries for three hours or more. You've lost track. It's late. It's the weekend tomorrow. You plan on taking the tapes back early before you head for that week's comics in town.

The following morning you're there again, tapes in the rucksack on your back, not long after the doors open. The workers greet you. They know you and the sort of things you rent. You know they tolerate you rather than are pleased to see you. After all, retail isn't always easy.

Once you have returned the tapes and made small talk, you turn and head for the door. Time to leave the video shop until next time.

You reach for the handle to open the door and stop. What did you just spot on the shelf? Is that a new sequel? You turn and look. That looks fun. A new entry in a horror franchise you like. Cool. You go over and take a look at the back of the cover. Hmm. Shall I?

Why not?

You nod towards the counter staff and they return that nod with a smile.

You're going to need another one to go with this tape for a full evening's entertainment. You begin once again to scour the shelves for your next hit.

Welcome back to the video store.

The secret extras at the end of the tape (Bonus content)

Think of this section as the bonus features, or even better, the *Videozone* feature at the end of a Full Moon VHS tape. Whenever I see a documentary or video on VHS or read a book about the scene, I want to make a list of things to check out. Presented here is a collection of lists that may spark some interest in seeking stuff out that you may enjoy.

100 sequels from the video era

I would hope that the pages of this book tell you that I love sequels in all of their often gaudy glory. I've got a lot of enjoyment out of them over the years even when their dubious quality had laid their franchises - and the careers of their casts - to rest. I have sat through more sequels than I could possibly count, sometimes several in one sitting, but some stick out as tapes that would always be visible on the racks in the video stores. Here is a list of 100 random sequels from the video store era that it's probably time I watched again.

1. A Nightmare on Elm Street 3: Dream Warriors (1987)
2. Halloween II (1981)
3. Aliens (1986)
4. Terminator 2: Judgment Day (1991)

189

5. Friday the 13th Part 2 (1981)
6. Predator 2 (1990)
7. The Empire Strikes Back (Star Wars: Episode V) (1980)
8. The Return of the Living Dead Part II (1988)
9. RoboCop 2 (1990)
10. Child's Play 2 (1990)
11. Gremlins 2: The New Batch (1990)
12. Poltergeist II: The Other Side (1986)
13. Hellraiser II: Hellbound (1988)
14. Star Trek II: The Wrath of Khan (1982)
15. Indiana Jones and the Temple of Doom (1984)
16. Lethal Weapon 2 (1989)
17. The Texas Chainsaw Massacre 2 (1986)
18. The Fly II (1989)
19. Jaws 2 (1978)
20. Blade II (2002)
21. Day of the Dead (1985)
22. Evil Dead II (1987)
23. Star Wars: Episode VI - Return of the Jedi (1983)
24. The Evil Dead 2 (1987)
25. The Terminator (1984)
26. Die Hard 2 (1990)
27. A Nightmare on Elm Street 4: The Dream Master (1988)
28. Friday the 13th Part III (1982)
29. Halloween III: Season of the Witch (1982)
30. China O' Brien 2 (1991)
31. Rambo: First Blood Part II (1985)
32. Nemesis 2: Nebula (1995)
33. The Mummy Returns (2001)
34. Mad Max 2 (1981)
35. The Karate Kid Part II (1986)

36. Back to the Future Part II (1989)
37. Critters 2: The Main Course (1988)
38. Return of the Living Dead 3 (1993)
39. Beverly Hills Cop II (1987)
40. Scream 2 (1997)
41. Escape from L.A. (1996)
42. The Toxic Avenger Part II (1989)
43. The Crow: City of Angels (1996)
44. Phantasm II (1988)
45. The Bride of Chucky (1998)
46. RoboCop 3 (1993)
47. Pet Sematary Two (1992)
48. Conan the Destroyer (1984)
49. The Howling II (1985)
50. Jaws 3-D (1983)
51. Halloween 4: The Return of Michael Myers (1988)
52. Child's Play 3 (1991)
53. The Fly II (1989)
54. Star Trek III: The Search for Spock (1984)
55. Poltergeist III (1988)
56. Tremors 2: Aftershocks (1996)
57. Teen Wolf Too (1987)
58. Fright Night Part 2 (1988)
59. Deathstalker 2 (1987)
60. Rocky II (1979)
61. The Naked Gun 2½: The Smell of Fear (1991)
62. No Retreat, No Surrender 2 (1987)
63. Demons 2 (1986)
64. Candyman: Farewell to the Flesh (1995)
65. Class of 1999 II: The Substitute (1994)
66. The NeverEnding Story II: The Next Chapter (1990)

67. Species II (1998)
68. The Prophecy II (1998)
69. Class of Nuke 'Em High Part II: Subhumanoid Meltdown (1991)
70. Creepshow 2 (1987)
71. The Howling III: The Marsupials (1987)
72. Trancers 2 (1991)
73. The Hidden II (1993)
74. House II: The Second Story (1987)
75. Beastmaster 2 (1991)
76. Puppet Master II (1990)
77. Pet Sematary II (1992)
78. Critters 3 (1991)
79. Hellbound: Hellraiser II (1988)
80. Children of the Corn II: The Final Sacrifice (1992)
81. Night of the Demons 2 (1994)
82. Hello Mary Lou: Prom Night 2 (1987)
83. House III: The Horror Show (1989)
84. Subspecies II: Bloodstone (1993)
85. The Return of Swamp Thing (1989)
86. Witchcraft II: The Temptress (1990)
87. Ghoulies II (1988)
88. Ghoulies III: Ghoulies Go to College (1991)
89. The Toxic Avenger Part III: The Last Temptation of Toxie (1989)
90. Sorority House Massacre II (1990)
91. Silent Night, Deadly Night Part 2 (1987)
92. The Boogeyman 2 (1983)
93. The Stepfather II (1989)
94. Slumber Party Massacre II (1987)
95. Silent Night, Deadly Night 3: Better Watch Out! (1989)

96. Maniac Cop 2 (1990)
97. The Return of Superfly (1990)
98. Psycho II (1983)
99. Escape From the Bronx (1983)
100. Scanners II: The New Order (1991)

Acting talent from the straight-to-video section

When browsing the releases that weren't the blockbuster type of films, you could be sure to see some familiar names. Those names would often tell you what a film's content would be like, such as in the cases of Shannon Tweed or Gary Daniels. Were they brilliant actors? Actually, many of them were solid in their roles, even if the films around them were less than stellar.

As such, here's a list of actors and actresses primarily known for appearing in straight-to-video movies in the 1980s and 1990s:

1. Shannon Tweed
2. Cynthia Rothrock
3. Don "The Dragon" Wilson
4. Michael Dudikoff
5. Wings Hauser
6. Olivier Gruner
7. Billy Blanks
8. Lorenzo Lamas
9. Jeff Speakman
10. Brigitte Nielsen

11. Gary Daniels

12. Michael Madsen

13. Burt Reynolds (had a period of straight-to-video films in the '90s)

14. Sasha Mitchell

15. David Bradley

16. Richard Grieco

17. Shannon Whirry

18. Fred Williamson

19. Andrew Dice Clay

20. C. Thomas Howell

21. Dolph Lundgren (although he transitioned back into theatrical releases in the 2000s)

22. Eric Roberts

23. Lorenzo Lamas

24. Traci Lords

25. Corey Feldman

26. Robert Davi

27. Roddy Piper

28. Bruce Campbell (primarily known for cult classics, some of which were straight-to-video)

29. Rutger Hauer

30. Linda Blair

31. Michael Paré

32. Corey Haim (in the later part of his career)

33. Corey Feldman

34. Casper Van Dien

35. Don "The Dragon" Wilson

36. Shannon Elizabeth

37. Mark Dacascos

38. Billy Drago

39. Tia Carrere
40. Udo Kier
41. Michael Jai White
42. Pamela Anderson
43. Steven Seagal (in the later part of his career)
44. Jesse Ventura
45. Stacy Keach
46. Martin Kove
47. Treat Williams
48. Lou Diamond Phillips
49. Sean Young
50. Robert Z'Dar

Rogues Gallery - companies that were known for releasing straight-to-video films during the 1980s and 1990s:

Much like the acting talent or directors, it was possible to gauge what you were in for simply by seeing which company were responsible for the flick you were holding. Here are some of the more prominent ones I remember from the rental era.

1. Full Moon Features
2. Cannon Films
3. Troma Entertainment
4. PM Entertainment Group
5. Vestron Video
6. New Horizons Picture Corporation
7. Trimark Pictures

8. Empire Pictures
9. Vidmark Entertainment
10. Republic Pictures Home Video
11. AIP Home Video (American International Pictures)
12. Prism Entertainment
13. Concorde Pictures
14. Republic Pictures
15. Hemdale Film Corporation
16. Shapiro-Glickenhaus Entertainment
17. Trans World Entertainment (TWE)
18. Fries Entertainment
19. Axis Films International
20. Carolco Pictures

Shopping list - Your next ten tapes

What will you seek out next?

1.
2.
3.
4.
5.
6.
7.
8.
9.
10.

Acknowledgements

Special thanks to: My wife Claire, my sons Alex and Joe, Rob Lane and Chris Annable at the 80s Video Shop, Gareth Packham at Video Tasties, Josh Schafer at Lunchmeat VHS, Gavin and Lucy at The Loft Movie Theatre, Zee Rowe at That Weird Shop, Derek Anthony Williams, Leanne Davis, Lee J Dowling at Tired George Studios, Mark Fox, VHS Mikey, Masters of the 80s, TheGebs24, Ed's Retro Geek Out, Fanzcene, Rob's Vintage Video, Old AF Reviewers, my parents for putting up with me and my friends on social media for not being sick of my crap. Yet.

Also by Andrew Hawnt

Across the Seas of Mind
Access No Areas
Diary of a Genre Addict
Dead Thing
For the Fallen
Bagged and Boarded: Life on Planet Geek
VHS Ate My Brain
A Stolen Fate
Captain Noize
The Damned Land and Other Apparitions
Nexus Point: Compendium 2020 vol 1
The End of Never: Compendium 2020 vol 2
Within The Beyond: Compendium 2020 vol 3
The Broken Dark: Compendium 2020 vol 4
Shards of the Infinite: The Compendium 2020 Omnibus
VHS Ate My Brain: Revised Edition

VHS Ate My Brain will return.